Lifelong Learners–
A New Clientele
for Higher Education

Dyckman W. Vermilye, EDITOR

1974

CURRENT ISSUES IN HIGHER EDUCATION

ASSOCIATE EDITOR, *William Ferris*

LIFELONG LEARNERS—
A NEW CLIENTELE FOR
HIGHER EDUCATION

Jossey-Bass Publishers
San Francisco • Washington • London • 1974

LIFELONG LEARNERS—A NEW CLIENTELE FOR HIGHER EDUCATION
Dyckman W. Vermilye, Editor

Copyright © 1974 by: American Association for Higher Education

Jossey-Bass, Inc., Publishers
615 Montgomery Street
San Francisco, California 94111

Jossey-Bass Limited
3 Henrietta Street
London WC2E 8LU

Library of Congress Catalogue Card Number LC 74-6738

International Standard Book Number ISBN 0-87589-240-X

Manufactured in the United States of America

JACKET DESIGN BY WILLI BAUM

FIRST EDITION

Code 7430

THE JOSSEY-BASS SERIES IN HIGHER EDUCATION

A publication of the

AMERICAN ASSOCIATION FOR HIGHER EDUCATION
National Center for Higher Education
One Dupont Circle, Northwest
Washington, D.C. 20036

DYCKMAN W. VERMILYE, *Executive Director*

The American Association for Higher Education, AAHE,
seeks to clarify and help resolve critical issues
in postsecondary education through conferences,
publications, and special projects. Its membership
includes faculty, students, administrators, trustees,
public officials, and interested citizens from all
segments of postsecondary education. This diversity
of membership reflects AAHE's belief that unilateral
solutions to problems are not as sound as those arrived
at through a coming together of all who are affected
by a problem.

Preface

This book focuses on lifelong learning and what it might mean to live in a learning society. It recognizes learning as a national resource and deals with ways to make that resource available to all citizens who need it or want it. In particular, the contributors to this book are concerned about the role higher education can play in lifelong learning. Several suggest that if higher education accepts that role and makes the necessary changes, colleges and universities can pass from the dog days into a new era. To restore flagging faith and flagging markets, these institutions will have to become inviting and useful to many persons formerly screened out or ignored: older learners, part-time learners, off-campus learners. These active adults have little time or inclination to adjust to the upper-middle-class youth ghetto we know as the modern university.

Historically, much of the change in education has been in response to pressures and demands from outside the academy. Among the pressures acting on institutions today are the relentless sweep toward an egalitarian social philosophy; the constantly escalating cost of goods and services; and the increasing needs of citizens to cope with change, preserve their identities against the massive machinery of contemporary civilization, and live meaningful lives. From an institutional point of view, these pressures might be labeled the access problem, the finance problem, and the goal problem. These problems are closely related, and to a great extent the future of higher education hinges on how they are met.

For some time, access was viewed as a problem associated with the disadvantaged and with the civil rights of minorities—youths who differed from the traditional model in skin color, scholastic aptitude, and socioeconomic background. It was a political and social problem of whether to let such students in and, once they got in, of how to keep them from flunking out or dropping out. This external pressure came at a time when most colleges did not need students; students wanted in. Now colleges and universities need students badly, and the question of access has pragmatic overtones related to institutional health and survival. And it is no longer even enough just to relax requirements and open the door. It is necessary to hustle, for many of these new learners need to be convinced that what they get out of college will be worth what they have to put into it.

Enrollment is one way that access ties into finances. Another way is in the systems needed to provide new students with learning at a cost the students and society can afford. Already not enough traditional students are able and willing to pay the tuition rates that some colleges need to stay open. The contributors to this book do not offer simple formulas for solving this problem, but they generally agree that significant new markets can be reached by broadening the concept of student and restructuring the ways students are served.

Solutions to problems of access and finance inevitably require a reassessment of goals in higher education. If the concept of lifelong learning has any bearing on that reassessment, it will probably cause a shift from institutional goals to learner goals. In a learning society, institutions have to fit students, not the other way around. Colleges and universities will have to help the student clarify and fulfill his or her own goals. They will have to recognize that the learning society includes a great many learners who differ in age, appearance, motivation, and needs from the traditional eighteen- to twenty-two-year-old college student. They will have to recognize not just one end of the bell-shaped curve of society but the whole bell.

The present usefulness of a meritocratic educational philosophy, in which the measure of a learner's ability is determined by comparisons between learners, is being weighed against an egalitarian philosophy, in which learners are helped in attaining personal goals and are measured by their own progress toward those goals. Higher education can probably not sustain itself on a meritocratic philosophy that is at odds with the society in which it must function. If it persists in trying, learners will probably find other ways and places to meet their needs.

The twenty-five essays included in this volume are drawn from the Twenty-Ninth National Conference on Higher Education, sponsored by the American Association for Higher Education. William Boyd, who was chairman of the Planning Committee for that meeting, shared in the editorial review process along with Harold Hodgkinson, Ann Scott, and William Ferris. My thanks to all of them for their help in putting this book together.

Washington, D.C.   Dyckman W. Vermilye
September 1974

Contents

Contributors

A. Nancy Avakian, mentor, Genesee Valley Learning Center, Empire State College, State University of New York

James L. Bess, director of planning studies, Research Group for Human Development and Educational Policy, State University of New York at Stony Brook

Linda Bond, codirector, Student Lobby, Associated Students of the University of California, Berkeley

Ernest L. Boyer, chancellor, State University of New York

Neil S. Bucklew, vice-president for administration, Central Michigan University

Richard Chait, director, Institute for Educational Management, Harvard University

George P. Connick, director of academic planning and codirector,

York County Community College Services, University of Maine at Portland-Gorham

K. PATRICIA CROSS, senior research psychologist, Educational Testing Service, and research educator, Center for Research and Development in Higher Education, University of California, Berkeley

DAVID J. CULBERTSON, president, Xerox Education Group, and vice-president, Xerox Corporation

HAROLD L. ENARSON, president, Ohio State University

ANDREW T. FORD, assistant to the vice-president for academic affairs, Stockton State College

AMBROSE GARNER, vice-president, Miami-Dade Community College

JAMES R. GASS, director, Center for Educational Research and Innovation, Organization for Economic Cooperation and Development, Paris

HAROLD L. HODGKINSON, research educator, Center for Research and Development in Higher Education, University of California, Berkeley

MORRIS T. KEETON, provost and vice-president, Antioch College

G. BEN LAWRENCE, director, National Center for Higher Education Management Systems, Boulder, Colorado

CALEB A. LEWIS, project director for *Courses by Newspaper* and specialist, Media Programs, University of California, San Diego

MYRON J. LUNINE, dean of the college, Hampshire College

Betty Jo Mayeske, director, Open University, University College, University of Maryland

John Osander, associate program director, Admissions Testing Program and College Entrance Examination Board programs, Educational Testing Service

James O'Toole, assistant professor of management, Graduate School of Business Administration, University of Southern California, and chairman, HEW Task Force on Work in America

Robert J. Pitchell, executive director, National University Extension Association, Washington, D.C., and chairman, Committee on the Financing of Higher Education for Adult Students, American Council on Education

Nancy K. Schlossberg, director, Office of Women in Higher Education, American Council on Education

John Summerskill, vice-president, Educational Testing Service

Robert J. Toft, dean of College IV, Grand Valley State Colleges

Wellford W. Wilms, project director, Center for Research and Development in Higher Education, University of California, Berkeley

Robin Scott Wilson, associate director, Committee on Institutional Cooperation, Evanston, Illinois

Lifelong Learners—
A New Clientele
for Higher Education

PART ONE

The Quiet Revolution

*A key word of the sixties may be coming back to haunt higher educa-
tion; that word is relevance. While the word itself does not figure promi-
nently in the contributions to the first part of this volume, there is a
strong consensus that higher education is out of joint with the times.
Not only the learning needs but the learning tastes of society have
changed; to judge from the migratory patterns of students in postsecondary education, higher education has not kept pace. Just as going
to college has lost much of its magic, not going has lost much of its
stigma. A couple of years ago, a television network put the problem
on the line with a documentary, "Higher Education: Who Needs It?"
For many Americans, the cynicism of the question was borne out by
personal experience.*

    *The authors of Part One are not optimistic about the prospects
of higher education, but neither are they cynical. These educators*

1

recognize that the wave of students created by the baby boom has passed and that enrollments are leveling off; the authors also recognize that the demand for learning—intermittent, recurrent, and lifelong— has never been greater. The opening chapter, by Ernest L. Boyer, deals specifically with the role of higher education in meeting that demand. He proposes that it is high time colleges and universities stopped serving as youth ghettos and started reaching out in new ways to new constituencies—or at least started to make it easier and more attractive for older citizens to use colleges as a learning resource. Boyer cautions against the practice—largely supported by the current postsecondary system—of slicing life like a salami into a chunk of preschool, a larger chunk of formal learning, a still larger chunk of work, and a nubbin of retirement. And he suggests that higher education might be revitalized both financially and spiritually by restructuring itself for a learning society.

James R. Gass and James O'Toole deal more broadly with the lifelong learning theme—Gass describing and giving the rationale for the European movement toward recurrent education, and O'Toole examining "the nexus of education and work" in America. Both writers see the need for higher education to become more flexible, more responsive to the recurrent learning needs of people throughout their lives—in a word, more relevant. Like Boyer, they reject the segmentation of lives into chunks of learning, work, and leisure. For Gass, the concept of recurrent education boils down to a question that seems to capture the spirit of Part One, if not the whole volume: "Will educational institutions (like the class structure) simply wither away in the learning society, will they find themselves faced with powerful and ultimately victorious competitors, or will the new clientele challenge them to renewal and change?"

As though picking up one thread of that question, David J. Culbertson, president of the Xerox Education Group, offers the challenging suggestion that one reason the corporate role in postsecondary education has been expanding is that traditional institutions have not met adequately the training and retraining needs of corporate personnel. Corporations have acted on the philosophy that if you want anything done well, you must do it yourself. Their experience to date suggests that this was not a bad idea. Corporate education programs— and proprietary institutions in general—are flourishing. One possible conclusion to draw is that in the growing competition for students, the formula for success may be as simple as identifying a need and meeting it.

Part One concludes with a look at students who make up a significant segment of the emerging learning society—those who opt for proprietary schools or enroll in postsecondary education as part-time students. In presenting findings from a study of the first group, Wellford Wilms explodes some popular myths about who proprietary students are and why they make the choices they do. In analyzing part-time students—a group that now actually outnumbers full-time students in postsecondary education—Robert J. Pitchell finds large-scale discrimination being practiced against them by state and federal lawmakers as well as by institutions. Both analyses provide much food for thought about the learning market.

In a sense, the learning market is what Part One is all about. The issue is not whether the market exists, but how to reach it and serve it. Resolving the issue will take change—not cosmetic change but profound change. Even so, the kinds of changes called for, some of which are already taking place, are not likely to make headlines. Changes inside that respond to changes outside, or changes that happen as the result of initiative rather than protest and revolt, lack the kind of sensationalism attractive to the news media. The learning revolution—and revolution *may not be too strong a word to apply—is a quiet one.*

WILLIAM FERRIS

Breaking Up the
Youth Ghetto

Ernest L. Boyer

Since World War II, higher education in this country has enjoyed both great progress and great good luck. During these nearly three decades, we responded to the avalanche of students. We built new campuses almost overnight; federal grants came pouring in; alumni fund drives often reached the top; and the shadow of McCarthyism lingered for a while and then faded from the scene. Somehow we emerged from these hectic, happy years with a network of colleges which C. P. Snow has called "one of the world's greatest glories."[1] We constructed more college buildings in twenty-five years than had been built during the three hundred years before, and the percentage of

---

[1] C. P. Snow, "Hope for America," *Look,* December 1, 1970, p. 34.

high-school students going on to college shifted from one in eight to one in two. I am convinced that when the final chapter of higher education has been written, this period—since World War II—will indeed stand as one of the "greatest glories" of our time.

Two things made all this come to pass. One was the nation's strong belief in education and the other was money. It seems incredible now, but in the mid-1940s this country spent only $1 billion on higher education—and today our yearly expenditure for all postsecondary education approaches $30 billion. At present, however, higher education faces what John Foster Dulles used to call "an agonizing reappraisal." The bulging postwar budgets are now behind us, the baby boom has subsided to a cap-gun pop, and there is a drop in college applications among the high-school population. Institutions across the land are cutting back, trimming costs, terminating contracts, and, in some instances, grimly fighting for survival.

What are we to make of all of this? What about the future? Some propose that it is time to fold our tents. The nation's colleges have passed their peak, they say—the glory days are gone, and we must now live with *retrenchment* and *the steady state*. There is much truth in this dark prediction. We do face a major crisis, and only the careless or the misinformed could be complacent. But, frankly, I'm even more troubled by the spirit of depression in our midst, for I'm convinced our problems may, at least in part, be self-imposed. We are becoming increasingly overwhelmed by the national mood of gloom and doom without generating new purposes of our own. And, most seriously of all, we seem to be projecting on the future some outworn assumptions from the past.

Our people are organizing their lives in strange new ways, yet our colleges and universities have not caught up with this social revolution in our midst. Let me explain this point. Historically, the span of human life has been chopped up into slices like a great salami, with each section having a special flavor all its own. First, there was the thin slice of early childhood—the time of happy play. Then came a thicker slice—twelve to twenty years, perhaps—devoted almost exclusively to full-time learning. Next, we had the still thicker chunk of full-time work. And, finally, came retirement—the little nubbin at the end—characterized by some as "dignified decline." In this traditional life cycle of the past, the stages of existence were kept rigidly apart.

What does all of this have to do with higher education? Very much, indeed, for throughout the years colleges and universities have conformed to this long tradition, serving just one slice of life. College catalogs and brochures were written for the young, suggesting that students come in just four sizes—eighteen, nineteen, twenty, and twenty-one. Classes were scheduled mainly Monday through Friday, usually 10 A.M. to 4 P.M., colliding head-on with the world of work. The academic year was broken into chunks by semesters, with time off in the summer so students could go home to help their fathers with the crops. Students were expected to finish college before entering the world of work, never to return. Through this process the campus became a place where older people seemed like misfits in a strange and foreign land. And adult students were viewed as retreads in a kind of salvage operation, sadly out of step with the learning cycle and even with the life cycle itself.

Through the patterns of our institutions, we locked this neatly ordered view of life into an iron vise of custom, and the campus became a kind of ghetto for the young. But now, all this has begun to change, and the implications for higher education are enormous. Consider, for example, the changes among the very young. Today about 40 percent of all boys and girls enroll in preschool programs before they go to kindergarten. Thousands now watch "Sesame Street" and "The Electric Company" in the home, and this means that the rigid line between the so-called "play years" and the "school years" is blurred.

The life pattern of older children has also changed. They now mature physically two full years earlier than did their grandparents fifty years ago. College students can now vote, and they have the right of legal contract in forty-three out of fifty states. And increasingly they leave college early or enroll for only part-time study, trying to break out of the so-called preadult stage of learning which seems to them a time of endless incubation. Incidentally, it is a startling and significant fact that this year over 55 percent of all those enrolled in postsecondary education are part-time students. Clearly the so-called college years are less well defined.

To add to this confusion, the tidy adult world is also beginning to break up. In 1900, the average American work week was sixty-two hours; in 1945, it dropped to forty-three, and today it is thirty-seven and one half hours. The shorter four-day and three-day work week is now also beginning to emerge. When the four-day pattern of a Massachusetts paint company was reported in the *Wall Street Journal* not long ago, it was deluged with inquiries from many companies, some of which have followed suit. People are less and less involved in earning bread five days a week, from early morning to late at night. Increasingly we face the baffling dilemma of leisure time.

One other dramatic pattern should be noted—the changing life style among older people. We hear a lot these days about how we have moved from a baby boom to a baby bust, but we should also begin to look at the opposite end of the population curve. Life expectancy has increased from forty-seven years in 1900 to seventy-one years in 1973, and by the year 2000 it is estimated that nearly 30 percent of the American population will be over fifty. Many people in these later years face early obsolescence. They are outdistanced by the pace of change and forced into premature retirement while still productive. This retirement pattern is not only wasteful, but tragic in simple human terms.

The point I wish to make is this. For years we have just assumed that life for all of us was neatly programmed. There were the early days of freedom; then came formal education; after that, work; then abrupt decline. And we quite properly built colleges and universities to fit this rigid cycle, serving principally the young and unattached. Now with the birthrate falling off, we are inclined to panic; we fear a new depression as we·lose our "natural" clientele.

But it seems clear that the old life patterns are beginning to break up, and that there is another way to view the present scene. The worst of times can be the best of times, to paraphrase Dickens, depending on your point of view. Even though the baby boom has slackened, there are still more people to be served. Mid-career people have more leisure time, and they face the crisis of early obsolescence. Older people now retire earlier, live longer, have more free time, and are often socially unattached. Now we have blocks of freedom throughout all of life, and for the first time in our history higher education may be viewed not only as a prework tradition but as a process to be pursued from eighteen to eighty-five.

Our job in higher education is to construct new educational arrangements to meet the changing social patterns. Let me introduce three concrete suggestions.

First, I suggest that we build more flexible schedule arrangements into the undergraduate years. Some colleges, even now, have a pre-enrollment program for high-school graduates, an arrangement which admits the graduate and then holds the acceptance while the student spends a year or two at work or travel before coming to the campus.

Related to this there is growing interest in the step-out program, an option which grants students a kind of leave of absence after several years of college before they finish their degrees. Such a move replaces the old dropout stigma which assumes that to interrupt the years of study is to leave forever formal learning. As colleges formalize in-and-out arrangements such as these, they simply face the fact that more and more young people want to pause, to interrupt the years of prework study, to go to college and have work apprenticeships as well.

I also suggest that, increasingly, we mix formal and informal learning throughout the adult working years. By this, I don't mean some vague commitment to "continuing education," a term we've spread like a musty blanket over all sorts of instruction for people over twenty-one. Rather, I mean recurrent education developed for specific groups of adult students to meet specific needs.

In New York, for example, there are fourteen thousand men in correctional institutions, and one thousand of them pass the GED high-school equivalency test each year. There is a great need for post-high-school education for these inmates, and the University is joining with the New York State Department of Correctional Services to open a minimum security prison where all the inmates will be also full-time college students. This is continuing education with a very special focus.

Another illustration of learning throughout the adult years would be our servicemen and servicewomen. In the United States, over 340,000 volunteers enter the armed forces every year, and many of these young men and women want to continue formal study. The development of a Servicemen's College Program to serve those stationed close to campuses, as well as those at more distant points, is a major higher-education challenge.

College courses for practicing professionals in such fields as medicine and law (to name just two) are another major challenge. In many states these people must now take refresher courses before they can be relicensed, and universities have a special obligation to offer the right courses at the right time.

Also, business and industry cannot be overlooked. Most employees do have more leisure time, and yet we're now discovering that the absence of work is not enough. With shorter days and longer weekends, workers often find themselves at loose ends. And increased leisure time often leads to fatiguing moonlighting jobs, taken not to increase cash but to head off boredom.

In his recent book, *Working,* Terkel says that unfulfilling work "may have touched malignantly the soul of our society."[2] Here again, the challenge to higher education is enormous, and I'm convinced that in the days ahead we'll have more education clauses in our labor contracts—agreements which will free workers to attend mini-courses or view video lectures during the working hours. And why should sabbaticals be limited to a minority of the academic elite? Why can't more Americans be freed at times to enrich their lives and refine their skills? Now France requires that workers in large firms after five years be given up to one year off at half pay for further education. Regardless of the precise form, it seems clear to me that in the days ahead the world of education and the world of work will increasingly intersect.

Finally, I suggest that we must begin to give more than lip service to older men and women. Sauna baths and shuffleboard for older people is a patronizing view of later life, and I believe these years can and must be a more productive time, enriched by formal learning. One campus in New York already has a residence hall filled with retirees, and another campus has apartments for people forty-five and older. With our empty dorms, why can't we join with departments of social services to help ease a pressing crisis—housing for the elderly —and, at the same time, bring back to campuses new groups of students, a kind of emeritus college on campus?

But neither should we write off the older person who cannot come to campus. If we can go into the factories, why can't we also go into the nursing homes and the retirement villages? Why should a person, after a lifetime of productive work, be allowed to vegetate intellectually simply because of the physical impairments of age? The individual should pay for learning, of course, if he can. But we have Medicare for the body; why not "Educare" for the mind? The cost would be modest, but the returns would be enormous.

In 1941, FDR inspired the nation with his "four freedoms." And now, as higher education's contribution to the Bicentennial, it may be time to add another—the freedom to learn—whatever one's age or stage of life. Such a commitment would reaffirm the age-old

---

[2] Louis "Studs" Terkel, *Working* (New York: Pantheon, 1972), p. xi.

proposition that learning and human dignity walk together hand in hand.

I recognize that as we seek to serve new groups of students, whether young or old, some formidable barriers must be faced. Internally, we'll have to build new courses, new schedules, and new attitudes among faculty and staff. I do not underestimate the enormity of this problem. And the problem of academic excellence will also come up. Some fear that more flexible programs for older people will somehow reduce quality, but I am convinced quite the opposite is true. Older students are highly motivated. They are often more diligent and more sure of where they want to go. It is a bit amusing now, but it is a fact that before the 1890s our public libraries were open only to adults. Children and young people were kept out on the theory that only older people knew how to treasure books and study on their own. I don't suggest that we reintroduce that policy, but we should at least remove the reverse discrimination against adults which still pervades some institutions.

Finally, there are those who feel that the greatest barrier to recurrent education is public apathy. They argue that more leisure time will simply mean not more education, but more beer, more baseball, and more television. Here again I'm convinced that this conclusion is contrary to the facts. Indeed, the recurrent education revolution has begun. Between 1960 and 1970, for example, the number of people engaged in postsecondary education shot from ten-million to twenty-eight-million students. Several years ago, when we started a noncampus college in New York, we were unsure of the response, but already the enrollment has passed two thousand and there are eight hundred on the waiting list. The average student age is thirty-three and the quality of the student is first rate.

One of my favorite lines is in *Moby Dick,* where Ishmael says of himself, "I have an everlasting itch for things remote." I am convinced there is in all of us an urge to learn, and it is unthinkable at this late hour in our history that education is becoming obsolete. Rather than beat their breasts over the new depression, educators should instead be looking aggressively for ways for people of all ages to scratch the "everlasting itch." Vachel Lindsay wrote a poignant verse which reads:

> It is the world's one crime its babes grow dull,
> . . . Not that they sow, but that they seldom reap;

> Not that they serve, but have no gods to serve;
> Not that they die, but that they die like sheep.[3]

The crime of life is not to die, but to grow dull and to "die like sheep." The continuous fulfillment of one's self—the avoidance of a living death—still remains a central goal of education. And this is a process which for all of us must never end. When all is said and done, education, just like the wars and generals, is much too important to be left only to the young.

[3] Vachel Lindsay, "The Leaden-Eyed," *Collected Poems* (New York: Macmillan, 1925); p. 69.

Education, Work, and Quality of Life

James O'Toole

Most Americans follow a path through life in which education is synonymous with youth, work with adulthood, and retirement with old age. Several problems result from dividing life into these discrete, age-graded functions. First, work, the badge of adulthood, tends to be regarded as the only fully legitimate activity of maturity. There is "something wrong" with someone who is not working, and the adult nonworker is considered to have and to be a social problem. Women who take care of their children, the unemployed and the underemployed, the dropout, the elderly, and even the adult full-time student— all lack full working identities. They suffer both economically and

This chapter is based on the findings of the summer 1973 Aspen Institute workshops on Education, Work, and the Quality of Life.

psychologically from their second-class status, and so are excluded from some of society's rewards. Second, research indicates that by segmenting life functions, we make the activities of education, work, and leisure less meaningful than if they ran as three strands throughout our lives. Third, family activities are segregated from other activities. In the middle years of life particularly, workers are separated from their families for many hours during the day. Finally, segmented life means that the individual often has only one chance for success or satisfaction. Only with difficulty can one escape from the track established by early educational experience. Those trained in vocational education shops, for example, are likely to be blue-collar workers for the rest of their lives—particularly if they are black or come from a working-class background.

The problem of segregated generations is related to the segmentation of life. Education, the activity of youth, occurs at schools, which become youth ghettos. Work, the activity of adulthood, is performed in similarly age-segregated institutions. Retirement, the activity of the aged, occurs increasingly in "leisure communities" cut off from the rest of the world, both spiritually and physically. One consequence of age segregation is that young people seldom, if ever, see adults at work. As James Coleman and Urie Bronfenbrenner have noted, this leaves youth improperly socialized to the work world and prolongs their adolescence. And cut off from older generations, from aspects of the essential guides of experience, tradition, and history, young people face a special difficulty in coping with important value questions in our rapidly changing society.

Giving rise to and reinforcing the problems of segmented and segregated living is a third major problem area—institutional inflexibility. Most schools are organized, by custom or by design, in an authoritarian fashion that instills conformity and obedience in pupils. They follow a model of rigid schedules, examination, grading, and set texts. Students go to school from 8 A.M. to 3 P.M. for nine months of the year, from ages five to sixteen (for the poor and working class), or from three to twenty-five (for the upper middle class).

Most jobs are organized in an authoritarian fashion built upon the ethic of conformity and obedience learned in the schools. They follow a model of set and simplified tasks, rigid schedules, and tight discipline and control. Most of us work from 9 A.M. to 5 P.M. for fifty weeks a year, from ages seventeen to sixty-five (for the poor and working class), or from twenty-six to sixty (for the upper middle class).

These forms apparently suit some individuals. But poor school performance and low work productivity are signs that something is wrong. Increasing numbers of people are demanding greater choice in the form of education: They are asking for self-mastery courses, flexible time schedules, and on-the-job and in-the-field training. More people want a greater range of curricular content, from pottery to phenomenology, from coping skills and risk-taking to Zen and the media. They demand greater flexibility from their jobs in educational opportunity, clothing, personal autonomy, and job design. And people want freedom to drop out of school and into work, out of work and into school. Surely a balance must be struck between complete institutional flexibility and maximal societal productivity, but at present the pendulum seems displaced too far to one side.

Finally, there is another cluster of problems at the nexus of education and work. These include:

Transitions. There are few institutions to facilitate the change from school to work. Exploratory jobs and apprenticeship programs are in short supply. Counseling, guidance, placement, and valid information about employers and jobs are inadequate. There are few (if any) facilitating institutions to help adults who wish to change jobs or to seek retraining for another job—although many adults demonstrably need counseling, information, placement services, and occasionally financial assistance. The transition from work to retirement is perhaps the most painful one in life; after over forty years of work, people are abruptly sent out to pasture. No attempt is made to smooth the transition by allowing the worker to taper off by working part-time before full retirement.

Transfers. Little or no academic credit is offered for work experience, and so workers, especially those in blue-collar jobs, have little incentive to take educational courses toward a degree. Employers do not encourage continuing education for their lower-level employees. And although employers often encourage continuing education for managers and professionals, such practice is discouraged for blue-collar workers if it entails stepping out of work for periods of over a month.

Credentials. We have required higher and higher credentials for the same work. High-school diplomas have become a prerequisite for most apprenticeships and entry-level, semiskilled jobs. But the economy has not changed rapidly enough to meet the requirements of the increased educational level of the work force. The expansion of professional, technical, and clerical jobs absorbs only 15 percent of the new educated workers; 85 percent accept jobs previously performed by individuals with fewer credentials. In some cases, higher credentials and job performance appear to be inversely related. Workers with high credentials quickly grow bored with unchallenging work, and it is among these workers that high turnover and low productivity are characteristically found.

Training. It is unclear when and where job training should occur. In the past, vocational education trained young people on obsolete machines for skills no longer in demand. Today, even with the best of intentions, there is an unavoidable lag between the time industry assesses its needs and the time when the schools can gear up to meet them. On-the-job training itself tends to be narrow, does not fall under any check for quality control, and the skills learned are rarely transferable.

Work experience. Cooperative education and work-study programs are widely accepted as the best tools for career education, but their spread is blocked by child labor laws, scarcity of jobs, and union contracts.

These are only some of the problems resulting from the delicate relationship between education and work in America today. There are other, equally important problems, including access to education for all age groups and all classes, access to jobs for all ages and classes, job and learning dissatisfaction, overcredentialing and undereducation, and more. This brief sketch is only a shadow of what could be identified, but I hope it will suffice as a prelude to several areas of opportunity that can provide leverage for dealing with such problems.

Clearly one area in which much can be done is improvement in fitting people to jobs and jobs to people. Although we know little about the causes of job dissatisfaction, the educational system has been partially blamed for allegedly raising unrealistically the expectations of youth about the world of work, preparing young people poorly for jobs, providing inadequate guidance, and mirroring the authoritarian world of work in its preparation of youth.

These assertions are problematic and deserve further study and debate. What is immediately clear is that each individual requires something slightly different from education and work to achieve satisfaction. As young people put it, "Different strokes for different folks." In conflict with this observation, we find that our work and educational institutions tend to be monolithic in their designs and in their assumptions about the capabilities of their workers and students, based upon race, age, sex, social class or educational credentials. For example, one consequence of this stereotyping is that employers often view blue-collar workers as incapable of tasks that require much intelligence. But there are over three times as many laborers as college professors with IQs of over 130. This evidence indicates that there are many very bright laborers in jobs that are unchallenging, dull, and for them often demeaning. It has been shown that these intelligent, dissatisfied workers are often responsible for defects, accidents, and errors in the workplace. In terms of the quality of life, it is clearly a waste of human resources to place bright people in dull jobs because we fail to recognize their potential. Such waste indicates the need to identify worker talent through more appropriate job placement, to broaden educational opportunities, and to redesign jobs so that they challenge bright workers. Particularly, educators might want to reexamine the system by which the sons and daughters of the poor and working classes are drawn into vocational education programs and thus set for life on a track that leads from second-class education to second-class jobs and often to social and political alienation.

Who should do the dirty jobs of society is a related public-policy question. We are beginning to find that our increasingly better-educated work force is less and less willing to do the vital but intrinsically unrewarding tasks of civilization. In Europe, this issue was not faced until Switzerland, Germany, Sweden, and France found themselves with an overskilled native work force unwilling to do menial tasks, and up to 40 percent of their work force composed of low-skilled immigrants who caused a variety of social problems. What are America's options in this matter? Should we open a national debate on our alternatives before we have a crisis?

We might begin by examining the pros and cons of (1) increasing the pay of those who receive no intrinsic compensation from their jobs; (2) placing the mentally handicapped in repetitive jobs they find challenging instead of placing them in institutions; (3) automating the worst jobs; (4) developing a public-service program to share the worst jobs—perhaps a year could be devoted after high school to such tasks; (5) offering workers a change in mid-career so that they are not condemned for life to a bad job; (6) redesigning the worst jobs to make them more intrinsically rewarding; and (7) increasing immigration. The questions of the fit between people and jobs underlie the central policy issues of job satisfaction, manpower planning, productivity, vocational training, counseling, guidance, and placement. This is a potentially high-leverage area on all the issues of education and work.

A second area of leverage is in the relationship between education and job success. Currently, it is impossible to trace the exact relationship between educational background and attainment on the one hand and future job success on the other. Evidence from the Coleman and Jencks studies indicates that there is only a marginal positive correlation between schooling and social/career mobility.[1] And in some areas the correlation is clearly negative. For example, entrepreneurial success is often found to go hand and hand with dropping out of high school. And Berg has shown a negative correlation between numbers of years of schooling and performance on certain jobs.[2]

But contrary evidence is just as strong. The increase in the number of black people entering the middle class has been matched with a concomitant increase among blacks in the numbers of years of school attendance and an increase in the number of college entrances. Moreover, almost all jobs for all people now require more and more years of schooling for entry level positions. This is overwhelming evidence, according to many, that schooling has become the indispensable condition of occupational success.

In short, there is much contradictory data about the relationship between education and job success. In sorting out what we know and don't know for policy implications, one issue is fundamental to our analysis: the market value of education. For some time, education has been sold as the means to financial and career success in life. Does the evidence support this line of reasoning? And even if it does, should the job-training functions of education take precedence over its value as preparation for family life, leisure, and citizenship? What should the educated person be? What will he or she need to be at the end of this century?

In addition to these important humanistic concerns, we simply do not know what the skill requirements for jobs will be in the future. Consequently, we cannot say whether education will pay off in the future in the way it has paid off in the past—that is, in better jobs. But we might begin our search for an objective basis for decision-making in this area with an analysis of the estimate of the Bureau of

[1] Christopher Jencks and others, *Inequality: A Reassessment of the Effect of Family and Schooling in America* (Basic Books, 1972).

[2] Ivar Berg, *Education and Jobs: The Great Training Robbery* (Beacon, 1971).

Labor Statistics that in 1980 only 20 percent of all jobs will require a B.A. degree for competent performance. From this, can we assume that some 80 percent of all jobs will require only the rudiments of education that are achieved at the high-school level? Or do we take our cue from other evidence that ties mobility closely to the kinds of training one receives and the number of years one is in school? Clearly, answers to the most pertinent questions about the future of education are hidden in the murky correlations between educational attainment and job success. To develop more meaningful public policy in manpower training, vocational education, compensatory education, and higher education, we must begin to clarify these relationships.

A third area where we can begin to resolve problems arising from education and work is in improving educational opportunities in the workplace. It is estimated that industry spends over $20 billion annually on education and training. If this is true, then industry spends nearly one-third of what is spent on education and training in the United States (federal, state, local, and private expenditures). Little is known about how this money is spent in industry. My informal discussions with educators and employers have identified several fascinating joint projects between businesses and educational institutions. But there is also a general feeling that industrial training programs are often narrow and not humanly satisfying. Some argue that often there is no linkage between training on the job and education in the broader sense. For example, training on the job is usually focused solely on learning a specific task; novices are not taught "how to learn" in order that they may later cope with change. They are often not taught transferable skills.

Some have argued that there might also be a basic philosophical difference between the goals of educational institutions and the training goals of employers. For example, the American formal educational system teaches two things: adaptability (how to learn, how to think critically, etc.) and conformity (how to adapt oneself to the requirements of organizations and society). Both of these are necessary components of education, but it is probably the case that training in industry is limited to instilling conformity. If this is true, it might suggest that schools should further stress adaptability skills to counterbalance industrial training. Then again, it might suggest an opportunity for educators to work with industry to establish on-the-job training with a more balanced curriculum and with standards that match those of formal educational institutions. In several successful experiments, colleges and schools have offered courses in workplaces. There appears to be an opportunity for true reform in education through expanding such efforts.

Another area that provides an opportunity to deal with work-education problems is certification and credentialism. Employers often note that a high-school diploma tells them only that its young possessor has served a four-year sentence in an institution. As a guarantee that he has learned anything, it is next to meaningless. But there have been some experiments with performance certification and mastery learning to certify that students meet various levels of performance in key subjects. There could be many levels of performance for each subject, and each individual could reach these at his own pace. Whenever he left or dropped out of school, the student could receive a certificate of his level of competence in half a dozen or more relevant subjects. At any time during his life he could return to school for instruction or testing in order to upgrade his certificate. This method has been suggested as a solution to a number of problems. Among others, these include meaningless credentials, competitive grading, sanctions against dropping out, barriers to continuing education, and lack of credit for noninstitutional learning. The possibilities of performance certification and similar solutions should be analyzed with the cooperation of business, labor, and education leaders.

Such an exploration opens up the broad questions of professionalization of education and work and the resulting thickets of credentialing, examining, licensing, and accrediting rules. Occupational groups have a strong tendency to seek recognition as professions and to define the educational requirements for entry into their fields. To examine this question raises delicate value issues—quality versus equality and consumer protection versus individual rights to mobility.

If there is an area in which higher educators will find themselves at odds with the long-term needs of society and their students, it is educational credentialing. In 1980, it is predicted that there will be two and one-half college graduates for every choice job. A group of educators recently proposed to solve this problem by raising the educational requirements for jobs. While this proposal might solve the problems of some educators, a longer-term analysis of the matter suggests that the issue is much more complicated.

These four areas—the fit between people and jobs, the relationship between education and job success, workplace educational opportunities, and certification and credentialism—might offer opportunities for leverage in improving the relationship between education and work. But what challenge to higher education do these issues imply? If I were prudent, I wouldn't try to answer this question. But I am struck by the deep sense of concern—even guilt—on the part of some educators that they are failing to make education relevant to the world of work. What is regrettable is that the ameliorative actions of educators in manpower planning invariably seem to make the problem worse. For example, when educators attempted to predict and meet the manpower needs of the nation in the 1960s, they ended up producing a generation of unemployable and frustrated engineers and teachers. Prediction from sheep entrails might be a better source of education decisionmaking than manpower forecasting. Since it is impossible to predict what the job demands of the nation will be in the future, one cannot, in the vocational sense, make education relevant to work. And even if these demands were predictable, what right has society to impinge upon the freedom of individuals to choose whatever career they want?

If one accepts these conclusions, one is inevitably drawn to traditional liberal education as the most relevant form of career education. All we know for certain about the future is that it will be turbulent and filled with unpredictable change. Historically, the people most able to adapt to the vicissitudes of social life have been the liberally educated. The person who has learned how to learn can always pick up a skill that has become essential. For the liberally educated, learning has always been a way of life. The person best able to cope with change is the one who has the broadest background and is thus the most flexible. I see no reason to believe that this will be any less so as the speed of change accelerates in the future.

I offer this disarmingly simple response from a statement in the Second Newman Report. In a laudable change of emphasis from their first report, Newman and his associates come out strongly for the values of education for self-fulfillment, citizenship, family and leisure, as well as for work. In this view, continuing education becomes the proper locus for specific skills training: "A more rational relationship between education and careers can come about if realistic opportunities exist for students to return to formal education on a recurrent basis throughout life. . . . This would allow the starting of a career without the feeling that one has lost one's only opportunity to insure social mobility through education, would allow an initial career choice without the fear that one has made an irrevocable life commitment, and would also allow a weighing of the value of varying types of education. . . . In the past the higher education community has argued eloquently for the broad value to society and the student of a sound general education. But behind that rhetorical front there has been a quiet argument for a second value—that of a college credential as a guarantee of a good job, high income, and social status. In asking the support of society, we believe that colleges must stand less on their value as certifying agencies and more on their value as educating agencies."[3]

Thus, to improve the quality of life, institutions of higher education should not look to be more occupationally relevant but instead should look for ways to improve what they have always done best.

[3] Frank Newman and others, *The Second Newman Report: National Policy and Higher Education* (MIT Press, 1974).

Lifelong Learning
in Europe

James R. Gass

In Europe there are now many signs of a move toward social institutions which recognize the inherent tension between individuals and society. The attempt to reconcile social planning with individual and group participation stems in part from a revolt against technocracy, for example, in the Scandinavian countries. The development of worker participation and control in France and Germany is an attempt to redistribute power in the industrial enterprise. Regionalization is everywhere pursued to push community decisions back to the local

The data and descriptive material used in this chapter were drawn from a series of studies undertaken by the Center for Educational Research and Innovation, Organization for Economic Cooperation and Development, Paris.

scene. The individuality of women and children is more respected in social reform. And the concept of recurrent education, which has forced itself onto the agenda of the European ministers of education, reflects growing demand for educational and work arrangements which respond more realistically to the richness and variety of individual lives. There is everywhere a demand for a more human pattern of economic growth that takes into account the satisfactions, as well as goods and services, that individuals seek as part of affluence.

Education should be the pioneer of this move toward a more individualized society. When all the ink has dried on the objectives of education, it will surely be recognized that the unique role of education is to be the bridge between the individual and society. It socializes individuals and also promotes the understanding that is the seed of change and even revolt. Education places the individual in the social structure, yet it remains the liberator from the existing class structure. Insofar as learning has become living—the leitmotiv of the report for UNESCO by Edgar Faure called *Learning to Be*—it should be continuously at the disposal of the individual during a major part of her or his life.

Far from being in the mainstream of development toward more individualized options in society, the educational system has pursued a strangely linear model of primary, secondary, and higher education for children and youth. Mass education has been construed as molding a bigger part of each generation into this same pattern, the frontier of educational progress being the age at which formal education for youth stops. The United States, with 35 percent of twenty-year-olds in some form of higher education, leads the field. In Europe, the same "end-on" model has led first to a major extension of comprehensive secondary education, followed by a vast expansion of the universities. New (and less onerous) structures of postsecondary education have become the order of the day as the strain on the universities and the public purse has reached the limit. But in itself the diversification of postsecondary education does not change the general pattern.

That particular bubble is now bursting, and it seems unlikely that Europe will follow the pattern of development in the United States. While it was practical politics two years ago to talk of extending comprehensive secondary education to age eighteen, it no longer is. This was an issue at the discussion of the European Ministers of Education in 1971—it was no longer on the agenda in 1973. But a different bubble is emerging—that of educational opportunities for people already at work. On a full-time equivalent basis, the Organization for Economic Cooperation and Development (OECD) has estimated that about twenty million people are now involved in part-time training or evening classes in OECD countries.

The central question in some European countries is becoming whether formal education and subsequent work-based education can be related as part of a coherent system of educational opportunities and responsibilities linked with new and more feasible patterns of working life and social participation. This, in rough terms, is the option of so-called recurrent education.

The core of the argument for recurrent education is to be found in an attempt to develop a new relationship between quantity, quality, and equality in education. Mass education must be based on a different overall pattern if there is to be any chance of reconciling it with quality and equality. Its protagonists argue that nothing less than a radical change in the relationships between the individual, the educational system, and the society will suffice to resolve the dilemma in which the "education society" now finds itself. On the one hand, society is compelled willy-nilly towards more education; on the other hand, it begins to recoil from the social implications of having an increasingly large proportion of young adults in institutions of higher education.

The basic flaw lies not in expanding facilities for higher education but in compelling young adults to enter higher education when their motivations would in all likelihood lead them to other social roles. It is a fact in most OECD countries today that the young adult who fails to enter higher education immediately on leaving secondary school embarks on a path of personal development that excludes the highest social, professional, and economic opportunities. Few people return to higher education after they have tested themselves in society. This situation might change drastically if young adults had a second option in higher education through the occupational system—that is, if those wishing to pursue their studies later in life would have opportunities equal to those doing so immediately after secondary school. It was done after World War II. Why not now?

There are many arguments in favor of such a radical transformation in the structure of higher education. First, in terms of equality of opportunities, it is surely the essential principle of democracy that the young citizen should be enabled to strive for his own progress when he knows what he wants. Second, a wider age structure in the universities would bring different forms of social experience into the student body. This change would strengthen the links between universities and society without yielding to the temptation, which is aroused in the present conditions, to distort the role of the universities as institutions.

It may be argued that the intellectual development of the individual is such that higher education will only succeed if followed between the ages of, say, eighteen and twenty-five. There may be something to this argument for certain disciplines, such as theoretical physics, mathematics, or symbolic logic, for which abstract, formal tools of analysis are necessary. But even so, the argument does not hold true for the majority of disciplines taught in institutions of higher education. Indeed, in many fields the possibility of fruitful academic study may be definitely enhanced by greater maturity and wider social experience.

The real terrain of argument is the socioeconomic feasibility of such a radical departure in educational structure. Is there not an unresolvable conflict between the income needs of the adult with family responsibilities and the possibilities of financing such a reform? Could career patterns be adjusted in such a way that a more flexible relationship between occupational experience and the educational system would be viable for the individual and for society? What would be the effect on the labor market of leaving school at, say, sixteen to eighteen followed by access to higher education between the ages of twenty-two to thirty and even later?

The response of European countries is of course varied, but there are some aspects in which the reforms envisaged differ from those under discussion in the United States. Whereas the main U.S. debate concerning recurrent education is in the field of postsecondary facilities (for example, the university without walls and the Carnegie notion of "age-, time-, and space-free" education), upper secondary education is also very much involved in the European scene. Second, the European focus is not so much on new education institutions at the postsecondary level (although it includes them) as on developments in industry concerned with educational leaves of absence. Third, in some European countries permanent, continuing, or recurrent education is looked upon as having repercussions for the whole of basic education. In other words, there is a tendency to look upon the problem as involving a basic structural reform of the whole educational system in relation to society—a new conceptual framework within which a whole series of related forms can be pursued over time.

This approach is illustrated by the following possible models for recurrent education outlined by the U68 Commission in Sweden. The concept of different patterns of individual development based on alternatives of education and work clearly dominates.

Model 1. Higher education continues directly from upper secondary school. A first period of higher education is followed by work in an occupation, after which higher education is completed. After some years in an occupation, a brief educational period follows, consisting perhaps of a refresher or upgrading course with some specialization.

Model 2. From upper secondary school directly to an occupation, after a period in which higher education is completed in one sequence. Refresher or upgrading courses are offered sometime after return to the occupation.

Model 3. Periods of occupational work both after upper secondary school and between periods of higher education. Refresher or upgrading course later, after some years in an occupation.

Model 4. Part-time higher educational studies concurrent with an occupation. These begin after a period of occupational work following upper secondary school. Refresher or upgrading course after some years in an occupation.

Model 5. Part-time higher education starts concurrently with occupational work immediately after upper secondary school. Final period of higher education is full-time. A later refresher or upgrading course may be taken on a part-time basis.

The reform of secondary education proposed by the French Minister of Education Mr. Fonanet, has somewhat the same orientation when viewed in conjunction with the Law of 1971 on educational leave of absence for employees. More varied education and work options for the sixteen to nineteen age group will be combined with the right to return to the educational system, including the university, for those who decide to work after secondary school. Such an approach to alternatives of education and work may eventually interconnect with the right of employees to educational leave, thereby connecting the formal and informal parts of the structure.

Taking the Swedish and French forms as illustrations of a similar general approach, what are the key components of the strategy? There is now a well-established trend in a significant number of countries—France, Germany, the Netherlands, Denmark, Norway, Sweden, and the United Kingdom—toward the reform of upper secondary education in the direction of more options and more relevance. The forms vary, but the basic common features are the postponement of choice by a common curriculum at lower secondary level, a broad range of optional subjects at upper secondary level, the fusion of general and vocational education, the strengthening of educational and vocational guidance, and the establishment of functional relationships with noneducational institutions to alternate study, work, and other activities.

Since one of the aims of the above policies is to remove the compulsion on young people to compete for university entry even when their motivations are in other directions, equity considerations require the establishment of the right to return to higher education. Admission requirements in many countries are being adapted to this need, and the development of patterns that alternate education and work is also facilitating the trend. A French secondary-school law under discussion specifically gives a right to return, but it is not yet clear how this right will be financed. Theoretically, it could be financed under the 1971 law on educational leaves of absence for employees, but so far this has been mainly devoted to short and predominantly professional courses of training.

Given the income returns to the individual from higher education, a logical step would be to give, say, two years drawing rights for everyone, more prolonged periods of higher education being financed by loans. Individuals could expend their credit of two years at various points in the life cycle, according to need. In some versions of the proposal, the drawing rights would cover alternative ways of using time, such as sabbatical leave, extended holidays, and early retirement. Such proposals are under discussion, mainly in the Scandinavian countries. A less ambitious approach to the same problem is a paid educational leave of absence, financed by the state and employers. A law to this effect now exists in Germany (1969), France (1971), Belgium (1973), and one is under consideration in Sweden. There is thus a rapid growth of educational activities devoted to working people (about 10 percent of the French labor force participated in such activities in 1972).

The above trends obviously mean a rapid change in the educational clientele, and there is consequently a rapidly growing need for "time-, space-, and age-free" postsecondary education. There are numerous developments of this kind, and in general they parallel those taking place in the United States.

An evolution of education as outlined above would transform

the educational establishment. But will educational institutions (like the class structure) simply wither away in the learning society, will they find themselves faced with powerful and ultimately victorious competitors, or will the new clientele challenge them to renewal and change?

The disappointing results in terms of equality and relevance of the massive expansion of the existing educational establishment in the 1950s and 1960s certainly gives force to the search for an alternative. De-schooling certainly has its charms and its inevitabilities, at least when it expresses the reality that all social institutions of the future must have pedagogical functions if the new learning and work patterns are to become a reality. But the aspiration that must be met is not only for continued learning taking place at and related to work, but for social mobility and occupational change through access to educational institutions. Recurrent education for adults should serve not only the needs for professional training, but also the need for educational, cultural and leisure activities for women and men caught up in the urban machine. Only if there is a new partnership between educational, work, and other social institutions could the new opportunities for individuals be made a reality.

The creation of this partnership is a dialectical process. For the advent of mass education is in itself bound to increase pressure for more interesting work, more participation, more social mobility, and, as a tool for all these, continued access to training and education. The claim for such access is now well-established in Europe, leading to legislation and collective bargaining between unions and employers. The outcome is a rapidly growing new clientele for the educational system. Of course, this new clientele will need new types of institutions. But it would be a great mistake if the schools, and in particular the universities, leave the response to others. The May 1968 events in France and those which followed elsewhere showed the dangers of a gulf between the universities and society. The most human and rewarding connection between universities and society—and perhaps the least dangerous—would be for universities to open their doors to students whatever their age. On this point, as on many others, Europe and the United States may have much to learn from each other.

Corporate Role in Lifelong Learning

David J. Culbertson

I was impressed recently with an experience I had in connection with a university advisory board on which I serve. We surveyed recent graduates of the business school, one of the finest in the country. Although the graduates were by and large satisfied with their schooling, one area of dissatisfaction leaped out—they thought that they were ill-equipped for the "real world." Among other suggestions, the graduates felt that they could have benefitted from more business speakers, more case studies, more computer training, and more learning of a practical nature. Much of this dissatisfaction is a result of the times in which we live. Students know that they can get at least some of the knowledge traditionally provided by the university from other sources—independent study, cassettes, the library, work-study programs, and even television.

This introduces one of the many problems facing higher education today, namely, competition. For centuries, we have looked to the university as the only source of post-high-school education. Not any more. Three of the largest corporations in America—IBM, GE, and AT&T—now offer bachelor's degrees. The Arthur D. Little firm has received authorization from the state of Massachusetts to give an MBA in management. In addition, more than two million students are currently enrolled in profitmaking institutions of higher education, and enrollments are growing rapidly. This growing competition from business strongly suggests that universities need to respond to the buyer's market.

Indeed, the failure of universities in responding to changing learning needs may explain better than anything else the expanding role of corporations and profitmaking schools in postsecondary education. For corporations and society at large have needs that for the most part are not being fulfilled by our colleges and universities—the need, for example, to cope with technological change. Traditionally, our institutions of higher learning have served as part of the pattern in which life is broken into three neat segments—the first devoted to learning, the second to earning, and the third to enjoying the rewards of one's labor. Clearly, this pattern has now changed. The engineer of today—to cite the most extreme example—must spend a good part of his life learning. If he leaves college tomorrow, half of what he learned will be obsolete by the time he is thirty.

Keeping up with technology is a problem not only for the engineer or scientist, but for all of us. The shift in manpower requirements brought about by technological change is awesome. Automatic elevators have displaced forty thousand elevator operators in New York City alone. New equipment in the United States Census Bureau now enables fifty statisticians to do the work that required four thousand people in 1950. The check-writing staff in the Treasury Department has been reduced from four hundred to four. Comparable statistics exist for the chemical, aircraft, communications, metals, mining, and transportation industries, to name a few. Americans have come face to face with a dramatic new manpower situation, requiring adjustments for which our existing structure of educational institutions and practices is not adequate.

Nor is the upsurge in the rate of change a temporary or accidental condition; it reflects fundamental social and economic forces that are likely to be with us for a long time. One of the most important of these forces is, of course, the progressively faster pace of technological change. Over a relatively few years, the advance of technology has created whole new industries—missiles, electronics, business machines, plastics, new forms of research. Brand new skills have been substituted for skills of traditional importance. Professional and technical employment rose 50 percent in the decade of the fifties and another 70 percent in the decade of the sixties—more than three times the rate of increase in total employment. New technology is squeezing the unskilled worker out of the labor market and putting a premium on ever more advanced training. Thousands of displaced workers must adjust to other industries and occupations to earn their livelihood.

Who is going to provide the education needed to cope with such change? Traditionally, Americans have relied a great deal on formal schools to prepare young people to enter the labor force. This reliance is fading fast. There is growing public awareness that the school system is not keeping abreast, that there is a wide chasm between the courses that schools offer and the training that people need for the world of work. While educators place a high priority on developing a student's mind and turning out a well-rounded human being, the public seems to be more concerned about jobs. There is growing doubt as to whether colleges and universities really fulfill this job-market purpose, and growing debate as to whether they should.

Leaving these questions aside—for they are questions each institution will have to answer for itself—I would like to turn to what Xerox is doing about its own education and training needs. Some of our steps are rather traditional. For example, we encourage our people to attend colleges and universities through a tuition-aid program that covers 65 percent of the cost. Last year, some four thousand people participated. We maintain a formal relationship with a half-dozen leading universities so that our people—particularly our research and development staff—continuously receive research reports, have the opportunity to attend seminars and conferences, and can avail themselves of campus learning resources. Xerox, of course, underwrites the cost to the university. We encourage—and pay the cost of—our employees' participation and membership in a wide range of educational and academic societies and associations. These groups run the gamut from the National Council of Teachers of English and the American Association of Publishers to the Information Industry Association and the American Association for the Advancement of Science.

But more important than these activities, it seems to me, are some recent developments that take into account the fact that all learning does not happen in traditional ways. Learning that is not academic is of utmost importance to human development. This recognition was part of the motivation that led Xerox a few years ago to embark on its social-service leave program, which enables some twenty-five people each year to take a paid sabbatical to work in a nonprofit socially oriented agency. The results have been most gratifying. Xerox people have worked in drug-rehabilitation centers, on Indian reservations, for the National Organization of Women, and in homes for the blind, the deaf, and the retarded. These workers have received at least as much as they have given, and they have returned to Xerox as better people. Indeed, the program has been so successful that we hope to announce very shortly a national program that will enable, encourage, and motivate all employees to participate more actively in their communities.

These kinds of programs foster learning of one sort. Another equally important kind of learning relates to the skills that help an individual do a better job and can enable him to move on to a more challenging and fulfilling position. For years, Xerox has placed a heavy emphasis on training and educating its people in this regard. Most of this has been done on a decentralized basis: sales training at Fort Lauderdale and Rochester, service training at five regional training centers throughout the country, management training at Exeter and other locations, and so on. A few years ago, we began to recognize that our training needs were going to expand dramatically during the 1970s and 1980s. As a relatively small growing company in the 1960s, we were able to recruit the people we needed from other companies who, many times, were doing a better job of training than we were. Now that we have grown so large, this approach is no longer feasible.

In 1968, Xerox had forty-five thousand employees. At the end of 1972, we had seventy-five thousand employees. And by 1978, we will have 135,000 people working for Xerox around the world. The figures represent a threefold increase in just a decade. Moreover, the technology that these people will be dealing with has grown more complicated and sophisticated. We have introduced several new products over the past few years and more are on the way. The training of the people who are going to service and sell this equipment has to become proportionately more sophisticated, intensive, and educationally sound. For all these reasons, the decision was made late in 1971 to construct a central training facility. The center is located on 2,300 acres in Leesburg, Virginia, a short drive from Dulles International Airport and thirty miles from downtown Washington, D.C. The first classes are just getting underway.

This training facility, which is much like a campus, points out that no matter how different the university and the corporation appear, they have much in common. Objectives of both university and corporation are similar. Each has a responsibility to enhance the quality of life. Even though the two institutions may use different means to bring about this result, they will succeed best if they move forward together, each learning from the other, each making its appropriate contribution—and above all, each recognizing that cooperation, not competition, is in the best interest of the people they serve.

Profile of Proprietary Students

Wellford W. Wilms

The ten thousand proprietary, or profitmaking, vocational schools in this country are big business. These schools enroll over three million students each year, producing gross annual revenues of at least $2.5 billion on which substantial corporate, property, and personal income taxes are paid. Cosmetology, or beauty, schools represent a third of the schools; trade and technical schools another third; and the business plus the correspondence schools make up the last third. Although correspondence schools represent less than a tenth of the proprietaries, they enroll two-thirds of the students and produce over half the income of the industry.

Despite their unavoidable presence, proprietaries weren't "discovered" by educational authorities until a few years ago. The reason wasn't that they were new, because proprietary vocational training began in Plymouth Colony in 1635 and later followed the dictates of the industrial revolution, offering training in merchant accounts, typing, and shorthand. The proprietaries of the 1700s and 1800s weren't necessarily "mom and pop" operations either. The founders of the Bryant and Stratton schools owned forty schools during the Civil War. Today, 85 percent of the proprietaries are owned by well-known corporations such as Bell & Howell, Control Data, Minneapolis Honeywell, and IT&T. How could such an enormous group of institutions escape the eyes of most educators for so long? One plausible explanation is that, in the early days, proprietary schools were conducted as businesses and run by businessmen and businesswomen whose interests centered on student recruitment and the bottom line of the income statement rather than on academics and scholarly writing. The interests and style of these business people probably eluded most traditional educators and offended the rest.

An interesting reversal has been taking place in the past decade. As academic education encountered rough fiscal sailing, it adapted many practices and employed people from the business sector. Academic institutions paid increasing attention to recruiting students, hoping for an excess of income over expenditures. At the same time, many proprietary schools have made a bid for "respectability" to attract more students and federal student-aid funds. In doing so, proprietary schools have become concerned about accreditation, transfer of credit, and degree status—issues that lay outside the pale of profit-making schools ten years ago. This merging of interests may change into outright competition as all schools scramble for their share of the student market and federal dollars. More information is needed by policymakers to guide the slicing of the pie. In what follows, I would like to present some interim findings from a study underway at the Center for Research and Development in Higher Education, University of California.

The study began in 1973; its purpose was to identfiy the characteristics of students enrolled in a broad sample of public and proprietary schools and to test the relative effectiveness of these schools in preparing people for employment. The study treated public and proprietary schools as conceptually distinct. Proprietary schools depend for their income on the occupational success of their graduates, whereas the public schools depend on the political process for financial support. The study was divided into two stages. The first stage analyzed the characteristics of 1,370 students close to graduating from fifty public and proprietary schools selected at random. The students were studying to be accountants, electronic-data-processing programmers, secretaries, dental assistants, electronic technicians and cosmetologists. The second stage, funded by the National Institute of Education and not completed at the time of this writing, is following 2,700 graduates of these schools into the labor market to analyze their success after controlling for differences in student backgrounds and characteristics.

Our findings contradict the popular picture of the average proprietary student. We found that these students tended to bring fewer resources to schools than students who went to public schools. Proprietary students were more likely to have dropped out of high school or graduated from a low-status general or vocational program than the student who chose the local community college or technical school. Also, the proprietary-school student was more likely to have come from an ethnic minority group, either black or with a Spanish surname, than the student going into public postsecondary vocational training. We found a nonsignificant trend for proprietary students to come from families of lower socioeconomic status than public students, and their verbal skills lagged behind their public-school counterparts.

Proprietary students generally had heavier schedules. A full-time program in most proprietary schools exceeded twenty-five to thirty hours each week compared to a full-time program in most public schools of about fifteen hours per week of actual classroom time. However, the proprietary student will finish his course of study much more quickly than the public student. While the proprietary student works fewer hours each week and earns less, he will be available for full-time employment sooner.

The proprietary student is generally regarded as a highly motivated, goal-oriented person willing to pay for fast training he could get free nearby. The study does bear out that this student has a heavier schedule and is more concerned with job success after graduation than the public-school student, but these factors are not strong enough to produce significant differences in the achievement motive of the two samples of students. Proprietary students appeared to choose their schools not because these students are more highly motivated than public students, but for other reasons.

The study indicates a tendency for the least advantaged students to choose the relatively expensive proprietary schools over the nearby inexpensive community colleges and technical schools. If public postsecondary schools are the latest extension of mass public education geared to the needs of the "new students," why do those students tend to pick the proprietaries? One reason is that public schools, when compared with the proprietaries, seem like extensions of the public secondary-school system, academic and middle class, to which many new students cannot relate. Despite the current popularity of career education, over 75 percent of the public schools in this study stated that their highest priority was educating students for life; training for employment was secondary. To meet this stated objective, the public-school vocational programs contain considerably more general coursework than the single-purpose proprietaries, which give top priority to training students for employment.

Also, public postsecondary schools often recruit their faculties from elementary and secondary schools, and this adds further to their distinct middle-class flavor. Katz and his associates, analyzing socioeconomic characteristics of the population of a California city, found that the local community college did not recruit the segments of the population with the fewest resources. They write: "The middle income groups dominant in the administration and faculty of the public junior colleges constitute its student body as well." Their conclusion is that the public junior college is more a bulwark for the middle class than a channel of mobility for the entire community.[1]

People who lack middle-class advantages, particularly if they are from ethnic minorities, tend not to participate in middle-class institutions. Recruitment patterns of the schools in the study emphasize this point dramatically. The predominantly middle-class students in public schools tended to come from high-status college preparatory programs and had superior verbal skills. High-school teachers and counselors helped guide these students into higher education at the local community college or technical school. On the other hand, proprietary students who made it through high school were more likely in low-status general programs and lacked the verbal facility of the students in the public schools. Proprietary students, who probably needed guidance from their high-school counselors and teachers, apparently didn't get it. These students had to rely on rather unconven-

---

[1] J. Katz, D. Gold, and E. Jones, "Equality of Opportunity in a Democratic Institution, the Public Junior College," *Education and Urban Society,* 1973, *5*(3), pp. 259–276.

tional sources of information, such as the Yellow Pages of the telephone directory and late-night television advertisements, to decide what to do after high school.

One reason high-school counselors and teachers do not guide students into proprietary schools is probably that these teachers and counselors, middle class themselves, feel more comfortable working with middle-class students—whites who have brought with them or acquired good verbal skills in high school. Another more pervasive reason is the real gap in information about the proprietary schools. When public-school presidents and directors were asked, "Do you feel that your school competes with other schools in the area for students?" only about half answered in the affirmative. When community-college and technical-school leaders were asked which schools were the main competitors, they most often named four-year colleges. None of these administrators named proprietary schools as competitors, which indicates a lack of knowledge. This lack of information is one sided, however, because directors of all proprietary schools said that other schools in the area did compete with them, and named local community colleges and technical schools as a major source of competition.

Contrary to general belief, then, motivation does not appear to be the prime factor that determines whether students go to public or proprietary schools. This study, which includes a wide range of schools and students, shows that differences in motivation determine the school choices of some, but not most, students. The issue seems not to be motivation, but psychological access.

Another area in which differences between public and proprietary students was explored related to their expectations after graduation. When both groups were asked about the highest level of education they expected to attain during their lifetime, both responded with what appeared to be unrealistic expectations. Almost half the students in the public schools said they expected to attain a bachelor's degree or more, and more than a third of the proprietary students responded similarly. These expectations are not a function of the amount of education already attained, because only 3 percent of the public students and 6 percent of the proprietary students then had bachelor's degrees. This finding is perplexing because neither public vocational nor proprietary programs are generally routes to higher education.

Students were also asked how much money they expected to earn three to five years after graduation and ten years after graduation. Many studies have shown that expectations change quite easily with feedback indicating success or failure. Following success, most people adjust their expectations upwards; after failure, most lower their expectations. Predictably, the students attending public community colleges and technical institutes, who had more resources behind them and were working more and earning more, expected more. On the other hand, students attending proprietary schools, who had fewer resources behind them and worked less and earned less, expected less. When we take into account the differences in current earnings by spreading the earnings effects evenly across both groups statistically, the salary expectations for each group become about the same.

The objective of the Berkeley study was to detect systematic differences between public- and proprietary-school students that operate across a variety of schools, geographic regions, and occupational programs. We did not intend to generalize about all proprietary or public schools, but we did want to demonstrate a principle—that public and proprietary schools march to different drummers (the public schools to the political process and the proprietaries to the market). This difference shapes the way the schools spend their resources.

Public schools, with their need to maintain a broad base of middle-class, tax-paying support, offer more general programs that appeal largely to the tax-paying middle class. Proprietary schools need to recruit, train, and place graduates in jobs successfully to get a return on their investments. Consequently, their programs are specific and determined by current labor market and consumer needs. Governed by the profit motive rather than political survival, the proprietary schools have a built-in incentive to seek out student markets not served by nearby competing public schools.

Financing Part-Time Students

Robert J. Pitchell

Part-time students have become the new majority in post-secondary education. According to USOE surveys, part-time students comprised 55 percent of the total postsecondary student body in 1969, and by 1972 this proportion had increased to 57.5 percent. In collegiate institutions in 1972, the number of part-time students was approximately half the total enrollment. Even more significantly, between 1969 and 1972 the number of part-time postsecondary students increased at a rate 2.3 times faster than full-time students, and part-time students in college institutions increased at a rate 3.5 times faster than full-time students. It is evident that we can no longer ignore this large group of part-time students in policymaking for postsecondary education.

Because there are several definitions of the terms *part-time students* and *postsecondary education,* let me pause here to define how they are used in this chapter. Part-time students include those taking less than the equivalent of twelve semester hours of undergraduate work, whether in degree or nondegree programs, and all students participating in noncredit organized-learning activities of short or long duration. Postsecondary education is defined as having four primary components: programs at collegiate institutions; programs at noncollegiate educational institutions; organized instruction at the postsecondary level in organizations with clientele groups that are primarily their own employees or members (for example, business concerns, government agencies, labor unions, and professional associations); and programs below the postsecondary level for persons beyond compulsory school age (this includes adult basic education and secondary school adult education).[1]

There are four broad categories of part-time students. One group includes those who are similar to full-time students in motivations and financing patterns, except that they are studying on a part-time basis. A second group consists of professional and occupational people who participate in postsecondary education because of salary incentives or licensing and certification requirements. This group includes teachers, police officers, doctors, nurses, engineers, and dentists, to name just a few professions and occupations. Among the nation's teachers, for example, 70.2 percent reported taking some type of part-time college study during the three years prior to a 1965–1966 survey by the National Education Association, and 61.1 percent reported part-time study in the three years prior to 1970–1971. In a national survey of noncredit professional-continuing education in 1967–1968, USOE reported that there were 921,015 registrations in a wide variety of noncredit programs for professional groups, of which teachers and other educators comprised 31 percent.

A third group of part-time students is made up of people who participate in education and training programs sponsored by government agencies, corporations, labor groups, and other organizations. These programs are financed by the organizations and are for organizational objectives. In 1972, USOE reported that 2,613,000 persons participated in employer programs and another 1,996,000 participated in

---

[1] Committee on Financing Higher Education for Adult Students, *The Financing of Part-time Students: The New Majority in Postsecondary Education,* Washington, D.C.: American Council on Education, 1974, p. 20.

programs operated by community organizations. Overall, 4,076,000 of the 15,734,000 part-time students, or 25.9 percent, reported that they were financed at least in part by their employers. In the federal government alone, almost one million civilian employees out of a total of three million participate in federally sponsored postsecondary education programs each year. Most large business corporations also finance educational programs for their employees. A 1964 survey by the National Industrial Conference Board revealed that 65 percent had tuition-aid programs for their employees. The Board estimates that the percentage is significantly higher today. And in 1969, a study by the U.S. Bureau of Labor Statistics indicated that 344 of 1,823 major collective-bargaining agreements contained training, retraining and tuition-aid provisions for union members.

The fourth group of part-time students consists of those recruited into federal categorical problem-solving programs. In 1972, there were 168 such programs with extension and continuing education components for professional and paraprofessional staff, the general public, or targeted categories of recipients. These programs were funded for $1.02 billion and included forty-five programs for the education professions, thirty-three for health professions, seventeen for social welfare, eleven for environmental control, and fewer programs for problems of aging, agriculture, business, community development, drug rehabilitation, humanities, law enforcement, manpower, nuclear energy, and science. Although the total number of participants in these programs has not been compiled, we know that agricultural extension alone, with an overall budget of $395 million in FY 1972, has a clientele group composed of much of the rural community in the United States as well as agricultural producers and marketers, and more recently nutrition aid and 4-H participants in urban areas. This agricultural-extension group totals as many people as all the full-time and part-time students who are normally counted as enrolled students.

At first glance, it might appear that part-time students are among the most advantageously financed of all postsecondary students. For some, the employer pays all educational costs plus salary. For part-time students in federal problem-solving programs, the government pays all or a large part of the costs. Still other part-time students, such as those in professional groups, are generally quite capable of financing their own continuing education activities, and their expenses are tax deductible. But not all part-time students are in such an advantageous financial situation. The evidence indicates that collegiate institutions and state and federal governments practice massive discrimination against part-time students, in spite of the fact that proportionately more part-time students than full-time students have a family income below $15,000 (72.4 percent compared to 62.2 percent, according to the 1972 Census of Population).

This discrimination takes many forms. The Basic Opportunity Grant (BOG) program is currently limited to full-time freshman and sophomore students. Even though part-time students are eligible for supplementary grants, they seldom receive them because institutions tend to make the supplementary grants part of a package of aid that is based on initial receipt of BOG funds. And while part-time students have been eligible for student-loan programs, these students have not been able to participate in proportion to their enrollments in postsecondary institutions: Only 6.6 percent of the recipients of guaranteed student loans since the inception of the program have been part-time students, and only 11.9 percent of National Direct Student Loans in FY 1971 and 22.5 percent in FY 1972 were awarded to part-time students. Furthermore, none of the $.5 billion annual expenditure in social-security benefits for the schooling of children with retired, disabled, or deceased parents has been available for dependents participating in postsecondary education on a part-time basis.

Part-time students do not fare much better at the state level. Of twenty-eight states with some type of needs-based student-aid program, only four—Connecticut, Maryland, Tennessee, and Wisconsin —provide eligibility for part-time students. In a recent survey by the American Association of State Colleges and Universities, public institutions in twelve of twenty-three responding states reported that no state funds were appropriated for off-campus credit programs for part-time students. And in a 1970 survey of its member institutions by the National University Extension Association, 46 percent of public institutions indicated that state appropriations for general extension and continuing education divisions ranged from 0 to 25 percent of budgeted expenses. Only Georgia is known to provide funding for academic instruction, research, and administration for noncredit students on the basis of full-time-equivalent continuing-education units, although Virginia and Tennessee have taken first steps in this direction.

Collegiate institutions contribute to the discrimination. Thirty-four percent of the 1,178 institutions surveyed by the Commission on Nontraditional Study in 1972 made no financial aid available to part-time students. Moreover, according to a recent American Council on

Education survey, 58.6 percent of collegiate institutions charge part-time students higher tuition rates than full-time students, with 66.9 percent of public institutions discriminating against part-time students in this way. Discrimination even exists in federal student-aid policies within the postsecondary education community. College students in certificate programs are ineligible for student aid even when their programs are equivalent to diploma programs at noncollegiate institutions. Finally, federal and many state tax policies allow deductions for educational expenses only when an educational activity maintains or improves an employee's current job skills. Thus part-time students who are ineligible for student-aid grants must pay taxes on income used as tuition payments in programs not directly job-related, while full-time students who receive student aid are exempt from taxes on their grant income, regardless of whether their programs are job- or career-related.

The deficiencies of our current system for financing postsecondary education are manifest. But what about the alternatives? Most of the current financing plans are student-based; most deal primarily with full-time students in degree or diploma programs; but many have recognized the need for financial support throughout an individual's lifetime. These aid plans basically fit into three categories: universal grants or voucher systems, entitlement-payroll tax plans, and expanded loan programs which include an income-contingency feature. Few proposals, except the wide-ranging Carnegie Commission reports and the proposal of the College Scholarship Service on the financing of low-income and minority students, take a differential approach to postsecondary clientele groups, especially as they relate to part-time students. No proposal gives any specific consideration to noncredit student programs. The proposals mostly consider the needs of students with individual motivations rather than students who are members of occupational or professional groups, participants in organizational employer programs, or in categorical public problem-solving programs.

To counter the formidable list of obstacles to the part-time student, I would like to propose five priority alternatives for financing postsecondary education. These alternatives are predicated on the fact that America is a highly pluralistic society with a highly pluralistic postsecondary education system which can best be served by a pluralistic financing approach. My first proposal is that postsecondary institutions, especially colleges and universities, should move quickly to equalize tuition rates for part-time and full-time credit students on a proportionate student-courseload basis. These institutions should provide eligibility to part-time credit students in all student-aid programs, especially in student-aid packages, so that part-time student needs can be met whether or not they are legally included in all publicly funded student-aid programs. Second, state and federal governments should include part-time credit students in all student-based aid programs. Governments should also include, in support formulas to public and private institutions, part-time credit students on a full-time equivalency basis, using the continuing education unit as an acceptable measuring device. The continuing-education unit is now a nationally accepted way of measuring instructional hours in noncredit programs and, as noted, is being used in the institutional support formula in Georgia. Third, state and federal governments should provide eligibility to part-time students in certificate and credit programs as a matter of right for qualified students and not as an institutional discretionary power.

As a fourth policy change, the federal government should increase rather than decrease its targeted noncredit postsecondary programs to achieve desirable social purposes. This should be done on a long-range basis for part-time students whose education and training would serve the public interest. Congress should fund the development of these institutional delivery systems for the same reasons it has supported agriculture- and medical-health-related programs. The funding of capabilities for extending institutional resources to high-priority clientele groups can maximize the targeting of educational programs for those with special needs at the same time that institutional strengths are reinforced and expanded. Experience with the Cooperative Extension Service indicates that this approach does not require massive governmental bureaucracies at federal or regional levels, nor does it deny the benefits of decentralizing programs to deal with local needs.

Finally, individuals and private organizations, especially employer groups, should be encouraged to fund their continuing education needs by private means or through tax incentives. Several major techniques for accomplishing this objective are currently available, including the adoption by employers of salary incentives for employee educational achievement; the enactment of requirements for continuing education in relicensing and professional certification criteria; special tax incentives to employer organizations to pay for part-time programs for employees at accredited postsecondary institutions; and special tax incentives to employed persons for educational costs—whether or not directly related to maintaining or improving current occupational skills.

In any examination of alternative financing programs for post-secondary education, I believe that the first order of business is to eliminate discrimination against part-time students. We should not wait until we have explored further changes in programs restricted to full-time students. The evidence already is in that the future of higher education lies increasingly in the growth of part-time student clientele.

PART TWO

New Ways to
Meet New Needs

The foregoing chapters provided a rationale and a framework for lifelong learning. The authors of Part Two zoom in on specific programs
and approaches that begin to tailor the learning process to a student
body as diverse as the citizenry itself. At the heart of these new efforts
is an educational philosophy that shifts the emphasis from teachers
and institutions to learners and the learner's place in life. As one of
the authors, Robert J. Toft, states: "If we could bring about a change
from 'what shall I teach?' to 'what should they learn?' we would have
moved a long way."

The eloquence of theory and generalization is appropriately
absent from Part Two. The chapters are short. This is the "how-to"
section and the authors are writing from practical experience. The authors are understandably enthusiastic because their programs, only re-

cently nudged from the nest, have flapped their wings and managed to fly.

Of all the chapters in Part Two, perhaps none strikes more directly at the heart of the learning process than A. Nancy Avakian's contribution on "Writing a Learning Contract." Avakian, a mentor at Genesee Valley Learning Center, Empire State College, takes the reader step by step through the development of the contract without losing sight of the fluid, almost improvisational nature of the process. One gathers that the actual writing of the contract, which requires close cooperation between faculty member and student, can be as rich a learning experience as the activities finally spelled out in the contract itself.

Keeping the close perspective, Robert J. Toft and Ambrose Garner describe efforts on their campuses to adopt performance- or competency-based criteria. Toft focuses on the specific problems and potentials of getting faculty from different disciplines to work together on a single performance-based instructional module. Garner gives an account of how performance-based thinking can be applied to an entire campus, including faculty, administration, students, and services. For both authors, the success of this alternative to traditional learning arrangements appears to lie largely in multilateral decisionmaking. Those who are evaluated take part in determining what is evaluated and how it is evaluated. Applied campuswide, this switch from unilateral, or top-down, education may be the boldest attempt yet at realizing the community concept of academe.

The last three chapters of Part Two deal with programs that go beyond the single campus. These programs extend educational resources and services to people who might not otherwise be able to receive such benefits. To take one of the Courses by Newspaper described by Caleb Lewis, for example, a person has only to subscribe to a newspaper that publishes the weekly lectures. The first course was carried by 246 newspapers across the country with 180 participating colleges and universities. An estimated ten million people read some or all of the lectures, and some five thousand took the course for credit.

In the pilot project described by George P. Connick, the idea again was to make learning more accessible. York County Community College Services in Maine demonstrates that through cooperation it can provide learning opportunities to those who have been passed by and can do so at a price the learners, the state, and the institutions can live with. The pilot project makes use of available facilities and the existing resources of public and private institutions of higher education.

In the final chapter of Part Two, Betty Jo Mayeske reveals how the Open University, imported from the United Kingdom, is working in America. The Open U., sometimes called the "University of the Second Chance," uses television, radio, correspondence texts, and learning kits to make higher education available to active adults who would find it difficult if not impossible to enroll at a traditional college or university. Three U.S. institutions—Rutgers, the University of Houston, and the University of Maryland—currently offer Open University courses. Mayeske describes how the Open University operates and reports on reactions from the first students in this country.

All in all, persons engaged in, starting, or exploring the possibility of learner-centered innovations on their own campuses should find these chapters on airborne fledgling projects a useful resource.

WILLIAM FERRIS

Writing a Learning Contract

A. Nancy Avakian

Many institutions now use learning contracts as a framework within which learning is described. At Empire State College, State University of New York, the learning contract is a term used to imply a solid commitment to a plan of study developed by a student and a faculty member after joint deliberation. The contract specifies the learning activities to be undertaken, the duration of the study, the criteria by which the work is to be evaluated, and the amount of credit to be assigned. The contract addresses itself to various dimensions of learning: the long-range plans of the student, specific purposes or topics, the learning activities to be undertaken, and the means and criteria of evaluation.

As far as they are able, students should clearly state their long-range plans, aspirations, or goals, for these interests provide a conceptual framework around which a sound degree program can be developed. The degree program, once developed by the student and faculty member, is approved by a faculty committee. In a sense, each contract is an avenue leading toward the attainment of the degree.

There are many conceptual and cultural frameworks which can help students focus their long-range plans. The major methods of study available to students at Empire State College are the vocational-professional mode, the disciplinary-interdisciplinary mode, the problem-oriented mode and the holistic-thematic approach. For example, one student's aspirations might be associated with the expectations or requirements of a vocation or profession. The major focus of study would be on specific job-related knowledge and skills, including conceptual foundations of the field. Another student may decide to concentrate in the area of a traditional discipline, while another may want to enter into interdisciplinary studies. These students must develop degree programs which lead to comprehension of the contents and structures of the discipline. One student may want to tackle a social problem, and therefore would need the knowledge pertinent to analyzing related problems and human concerns. Or there may be a student interested in organizing work around a major theme that has its own conceptual complexities and integrity.

The student who is uncertain about future directions or who has had limited academic experience may wish to explore different areas by way of short investigatory contracts before deciding on a major area of concentration. These short contracts help the student learn how to work independently in a relatively new mode. They give the student and faculty member a chance to assess the student's ability and level of academic competence. Short contracts also help the student clarify his interests and purposes.

The specific purposes of a learning contract pertain to the topics or themes to be covered in one contract. In addition to relating to the degree program, the topics could be linked with appropriate learning resources: independent studies, modules, work internships, formal coursework, residency programs, travel, or research. For example, a student might wish to pusue independent study somewhat in the manner of a correspondence course, working through a study guide and required reading in textbooks, journals, and other resource books. The State University of New York has a series of independent studies usually equivalent to a three-hour course taken at a traditional institution. There are approximately ninety independent study guides in over thirty areas of study. Many of these are supplemented with films, video tapes, audio cassettes, slides, or laboratory kits. There are also courses offered by industry or by community agencies; others are carried by way of radio, television, and the newspaper. The source and the medium are less important than the appropriateness of the independent study as determined by the student and faculty member developing the contract.

Rather than pursue independent studies, some students may wish to work through modules—short discourses designed to encourage and stimulate students to develop their interests or undertake research. Empire State College has developed a series of these modules ranging from a study of witchcraft in America to a determination of the scientific aspects of music. Usually there are no programmed texts attached to the modules, but many thought-provoking questions are stimulated.

As a third alternative, a student might wish to serve an internship connected with a job, making the work a part of the learning activity. One student at Empire State College worked as an administrative assistant to a superintendent at the Board of Cooperative Educational Services. As part of her job, she was to help develop a curriculum for teaching personal hygiene to mentally retarded teenagers. The superintendent, who served as her tutor, suggested a bibliography, discussed the curriculum objectives, and worked with her daily. Even though the development of a curriculum was part of her work, it definitely was a learning experience for her. Other students may work as interns in government or social agencies, theaters, museums, radio or television studios, laboratories, libraries, or any number of settings. If the work supervisor is to act as the student's tutor, the responsibilities of the role should be agreed upon and outlined in the learning contract. The actual learning components of the field work, as well as the evaluative criteria, must also be specified in the contract.

Another type of learning resource is the tutor. This alternative might suit the student who wishes to study in an area where the faculty member does not have competence. For example, a student who is interested in designing and repairing stringed instruments might work with an artisan who agrees to be the tutor. An agreement must be reached whereby the learning activities, the number of contact hours, the expected outcomes, and the evaluative criteria are detailed by the student, the artisan, and the faculty member before the student undertakes the work.

For students who need interaction with other students, a learning contract can be written in which the student enrolls in a formal course or courses at another institution. On the other hand, a collective contract involving many students might be designed with one or more faculty members participating. Each student could pursue part of the contract and at the same time share in the breadth and depth of the entire undertaking. Another method of fostering this type of interaction is a cooperative study in which a group of students explore a common interest. Such a study may evolve into a residency program in which students meet for a week or an occasional long weekend to share experiences, products, and insights, or sharpen skills and concepts. Workshops and conferences with visiting and residential scholars can be scheduled. The particular facilities used for such residencies need not be elaborate; a temporarily vacated college dormitory would do as would an old house in the country or an off-season motel. A residential program in the arts, sponsored by Empire State College, took place at the Skidmore College campus in Saratoga Springs, New York, so that participants could also attend the performances and cultural events at the Saratoga Performing Arts Center. The residency was about eight days. The facilities were not the significant factor; the important objective was to bring together people with like interests so they might create for themselves while they were there.

Travel, an important element of education, might also be included in a contract—not the travel per se, but the actual programs and activities undertaken during the trip. Such activities could include living with a family in a foreign country, visiting historical sites, attending cultural events, studying trade unions, or participating in archeological digs. One student, who was involved in a study of nursery-school programs, decided two weeks into the contract that she would accompany her husband to England on a business trip for ten days. Rather than withdraw from her studies or prolong the time element of the learning contract, she and the faculty member working with her amended the learning contract to incorporate the trip. While in England, she visited several nursery schools and interviewed the parents of children in these schools. In a later learning contract, she interviewed parents of children in nursery schools in this country and did a comparative study with the information she had obtained in England.

Any combination of the foregoing approaches may be written into a single contract. For example, a student enrolled in a child psychology course might simultaneously have a field experience as a volunteer worker in the children's ward of a local hospital, combining theory with practical experience. The numerous ways of combining activities depend on the time involved, the resources available, and the needs of the student. Of course, not to be overlooked is a contract where a faculty member works directly with a student who is pursuing a particular competence or undertaking independent research.

There follow some questions the student and faculty member might want to keep in mind when stating the purposes of the contract: What will be the end result of this contract? Will it be a behavior, a product, or a process? Will the outcome relate to the terms of the student's long-range plans? Is the student equipped to achieve the stated goals within the time limits of the contract? Are there opportunities for the student to pursue these goals? Will an informed observer such as a work supervisor, a tutor, a field worker, or a consultant be able to help the student achieve the expected outcome?

The third part of a contract, the learning activity, must be specific. If particular books are to be read, they should be listed. If a student is going to develop a bibliography, this should be indicated. If a student is to choose from several alternatives, these should be mentioned. For example, a learning contract can indicate that the student has a choice of writing a case study or doing in-depth research on one aspect of an area. Both should be mentioned as alternatives. If individuals are to be interviewed, their names, offices, and responsibilities should be indicated as well as the purpose of the interviews. When field trips or volunteer activities are anticipated, the when, where, with whom and for what should be mentioned. Meetings of students with faculty members or tutors should be specified by time and purpose, even if the purpose is only to create check points for progress reports. Dates for submission of papers or examinations should also be included. Finally, if a student is going to enroll in a class at another institution, the title of the course, the catalog number and, if possible, a course description should be included.

The learning activities should be specific enough for the student to proceed and yet sufficiently flexible to permit initiative and creativity. The student can record activities pertinent to learning in a log book. Again, the log should be specific, naming individuals contacted, recording bibliography, and mentioning events attended, facilities visited, or field work accomplished. It is important that the log also identify significant ideas encountered by the student. Through a log, both student and faculty member can analyze the cumulative value of the activities, their contribution to the student's degree program, and their implications for future studies. A log need not, and indeed should not, be a diary or intimate revelation of personal matters.

Learning contracts should be explicit about evaluation and the criteria to be applied. Is the process of learning to be stressed? Are special techniques to be mastered? What ideas or concepts are anticipated? Is the objective of this learning contract concerned with the student's ability to analyze and criticize a concept or to synthesize it and indicate its application to a relevant situation? Whatever is to be evaluated should be specified: a paper, a log, a journal, work samples, an oral presentation, an artistic performance, or a test.

Each institution has its own method of recording evaluations. At Empire State College, a digest and evaluation of a learning contract includes a restatement of the objectives of the learning contract, the learning activities, the criteria which were established for the evaluation, and the actual evaluation. This may be a grade which appears on the transcript of another institution where the student enrolled in a course. More often, it is a description of the techniques a student mastered or the application of a concept to a pertinent situation. Usually the student's growth and strengths are identified as well as areas that need improvement.

The duration of a learning contract should be indicated with a beginning date and an ending date. It might be helpful to equate the learning activities of a one-month contract with a four-hour course at a traditional institution. It is conceivable that a student may want to explore alternative resources or to prepare a bibliography which is to be included in a learning contract. In such a case, the actual writing of a learning contract might be delayed. When it is written, it might be backdated to include the student's work. This kind of flexibility is important. Even though the assumption is that careful planning precludes major changes in the execution of the contract, a student in consultation with the faculty member should be able to modify a contract for sufficient reason. Therefore, provisions for amending a contract should be available.

Contracts should clearly indicate the responsibilities of the faculty member or tutor as well as those of the student. At Empire State College, after a learning contract has been signed by the student and faculty member it is reviewed and signed by the associate dean of the learning contract and then read by the office of the vice president for academic affairs. This review process seems relatively simple compared to the opportunities, challenges, and excitement of working via the learning contract. Or perhaps more accurately stated, the contractual mode provides an individualized approach to learning which is the essence of education.

Designing a Module

Robert J. Toft

Any discussion of designing a single performance-based module immediately raises two conflicts. The first conflict arises out of the difference between preparing materials for teaching and preparing materials for learning. The second conflict arises between strict discipline orientation and interdisciplinary, cross-disciplinary, or nondisciplinary work. I would like to deal briefly with the problems of teaching-centered versus learning-centered materials first, then move on to the problems and potentials of integrating discipline-oriented materials.

Because of my interest in modular instruction, I have been asked if I foresee some sort of module revolution for American undergraduate education. My answer is an emphatic no. Every curriculum has areas in which learning modules that can be studied independently

57

will be of great value. Modules work very well for selective remediation in skills such as reading, writing, and mathematics, and are also useful for representing relatively esoteric areas where the clientele will be small. But I don't see modules replacing lectures throughout our colleges and universities. Rather, I think a far more reasonable and worthwhile goal would be raising the consciousness of undergraduate faculties to recognize the value of setting explicit objectives for the materials they teach. If all faculty members analyzed their course materials from the standpoint of deciding what their students must know, and if they then arranged the materials to truly facilitate student learning, it would not matter whether the materials were delivered by lecture, discussion, tutorial, or whatever method. If we could bring about a change from "what shall I teach?" to "what should they learn?" we would have moved a long way.

The second conflict area—that of integrating discipline-oriented materials—can only be resolved through faculty cooperation. From the standpoint of the curriculum, one of the major reasons faculty need to cooperate in the design of modules is to eliminate repetition. In a study of the engineering curriculum at UCLA in the mid-1960s, for example, a 40 percent repetition was found in the teaching of mathematical concepts. Most professors spent a lot of time going over previously plowed ground. For many students the review was worthwhile, but for others it was a waste of time. When the curriculum was analyzed and this repetition was found, packages containing the prerequisite mathematics were developed and made available to the students. If students needed to review, the onus was on them to do so. In our own curriculum at College IV of Grand Valley State Colleges, both the chemistry sequence and the biology sequence had a module on the metric system. These two have now been combined into a single module.

There are two other areas in which faculty cooperation is needed in the development of modules. The first is where there are natural bridges between two or more disciplines, such as between psychology and sociology. Common modules representing a hybrid of two or more areas can be developed to enrich the curriculum. Second, faculty cooperation is needed when several disciplines are relevant to one issue, such as eugenics or an environmental problem. A group of faculty may well put together one or more modules on a topic such as poverty and may give it a problem-solving focus.

To create modules in any of these areas, the faculty participants must make a few preliminary decisions. Faculty must first decide on the scope of the module. The tendency is to let the module grow out of some informal discussions and quickly find that it encompasses far too much to be practical. A limit has to be set on the estimated effort to be required of the student. Second, the group must agree on the objective of the module. This is sometimes quite difficult because an interdisciplinary module involves several independent viewpoints. Usually, stating a single comprehensive objective for the module requires a compromise on the part of all participants. In many cases, each participant must learn something more about the discipline of colleagues before an agreement can be reached. This is, of course, one of the more exciting aspects of such an exercise.

The group must then select the essential materials from all the disciplines involved. The key word here is *essential*. It is easy to put together enough materials for a large textbook in a module that may carry one credit. In this respect one has to guard against the sin of pride; a natural tendency exists to want to show your colleagues that you really "know your stuff." Selectivity coupled with humility should be the order.

The next problem is to remove the disciplinary biases of the participating faculty. At this stage, the territorial imperative inappropriately appears and a breakdown in communication often occurs. Each participant is convinced that the material cannot be presented without the trappings of his particular discipline. A further argument used is that to remove materials that are considered fundamental by the proponent and superfluous by the other team members results in a dull, sterile module. As this unproductive discussion continues, the telling blow is usually delivered in words to this effect: "Well, this module would not be acceptable to me and my colleagues for credit in our department." To get beyond this point, a tactic often used successfully is that of placing the discipline-oriented trappings in a series of introductory comments or statements leading into the module. In this way, the module may be cleansed, thus protecting its original objective, and the consciences of the participants will be clear because they have preserved those elements considered to be essential prerequisites.

The faculty are then ready to begin the actual writing. A working outline should be constructed and sections assigned to participants. After an initial draft is complete, it should be read and criticized by all. This is a tough job and insecurities pop up, but good will and constructive criticism help a great deal. The format of the module may be left until the first materials are seen. In general, a useful module will begin with a rationale that lets the student understand the reason for learning the material. There should be a clear objective stated in terms that allow both the student and tester to have a definite end point in mind. Avoid such fuzzies as "the student will appreciate . . . understand . . . to be aware of," and so on. Ask for a performance that is measurable. The objective is followed by the study guide and list of student activities involved in learning the material. Finally, a self-assessment should be provided for the student. This serves as a test of learning, a reminder to restudy that which is not clear, and a positive reinforcer when used with the mastery exam.

The use of media other than the printed word is an important consideration. My view is that the material should dicate the media and not the reverse. With the costs of media varying over an enormous range, one should be selective in choosing the appropriate medium to best present the message, but keep in mind that the message is the most important.

It is best to do a trial version of the module for use first and to be explicit in stating that the material is preliminary. This trial version encourages colleagues and students to give constructive advice and criticisms, and also reduces the natural anxiety of putting one's name in print. Use students as creators, writers, and consumers of the module. Their contributions are valuable and their particular orientation as learners will help eliminate many pitfalls. Students will put forth enormous effort to do excellent creative work. When they do, they should be rewarded with an acknowledgement or coauthorship.

At this point I want to stress that the form of a module ought to be variable and will be dictated somewhat by the materials available for inclusion. The simplest module to construct is one containing an objective, a rationale, a study guide keyed to a standard textbook, and a self-assessment procedure. To be effective, the study guide must do more than list chapter and verse. It must be thought out carefully to call attention to important points, obscure facts, and potential roadblocks. A second type of module is one in which the study guide incorporates some reprints or other commercial material and some original writing. Obviously, this type requires more effort to construct, but is often more satisfying to both the faculty member and the student. A third type of module is one totally constructed by the faculty member. This contains all original writing and is a massive effort. Needless to say, time constraints often dictate that preliminary editions are of types one and two and later editions are of type three. In modules designed by a committee, the second type, incorporating both original and secondary material, will most likely be used.

In order for innovation and growth of the curriculum to be sustained, there must be institutional commitment at the highest levels. Without positive and continued support from the president, vice president, and dean, there will be only sporadic and largely ineffective attempts at real change. The goals of the institution must be such that creativity and innovation are recognized, respected, and rewarded.

Although there are many ways administrators can foster creativity and innovation, I will mention only three. In the budgetmaking process, provisions should be made so that each unit, whether a department or a school, has some available venture capital. In times of tight budgets, this capital is a difficult proposition, but one that is absolutely essential. Such discretionary funds, even if small, can have a great multiplier effect when combined with the willing contribution of time from dedicated faculty. A second way to foster innovation is to set aside for the unit a portion of the indirect costs resulting from any grants initiated by that unit. This provides a real incentive to find outside support for the innovative activities of a department or school. Third, and most important in the long run, is the necessity of developing policies for faculty retention and promotion which include recognition of scholarly and innovative contributions to the instructional program.

Performance-Based Campus

Ambrose Garner

The literature of professional education today abounds with terms such as *behavioral objectives, performance objectives, competency-based education, measurable objectives, systems approaches to education, management by objectives,* and *administration through objectives.* While some vestiges of common meaning exist within the various terminologies, great confusion also exists. Vagueness and ambiguity plague the language of performance-based education. Referents of words and phrases are frequently obscured, and the phraseology generally fails to indicate the scope of the educational enterprise under discussion. Any attempt to develop or describe the performance-based college campus involves a complex challenge and a rare opportunity.

It is a challenge in the sense that, at least in the judgment of some, no such organization has been developed, and an opportunity in the sense that the relatively short history of performance-based education allows for almost complete freedom in design and development of a system. The challenge is real and complex enough to be awe-inspiring.

Despite the long history of education, there are still three important questions about the educational enterprise that have been left unanswered: What changes are sought in the behavior of students? How are those changes to be achieved? And how are teachers to know when the changes have been achieved? If we ask the typical college faculty member what objectives he is trying to achieve, he will very likely provide us with a description of the activities in which he engages. This confusion of strategies with objectives is one of the major reasons that it is so difficult to achieve meaningful changes in the educational system. If a faculty member equates his strategies with his objectives, then discussion of possible changes in education implies changes in his strategies. This, in turn, may be interpreted as criticism of his performance or as a threat to his academic freedom. If, however, differentiation between strategies and objectives has been accomplished and the terms clearly defined, then faculty activities can be assessed in terms of their relative efficacy in achieving the stated objectives.

While educators may agree that the age of accountability has arrived, they do not agree on the wisdom of producing a performance-based system of higher education. Perhaps the issues are nowhere more clearly illustrated than in the February, 1972, issue of *Educational Leadership* in which Gagne presents an article entitled "Behavioral Objectives? Yes!" and Kneller responds with an article entitled "Behavioral Objectives? No!" Gagne contends that the statement of behavioral objectives is necessary in order to communicate expectations to students, to enhance design of the educational experience, and to evaluate the outcomes of the educational enterprise. Kneller contends, "This approach to instruction rests on assumptions about human behavior that are reductionist, deterministic, and physicalist. It is opposed to the view that learning is self-directed, unstructured, and in large part unpredictable." Kneller concludes that the program of the behavior objectivist has very little place in education.

Analyzing these opposing viewpoints, those who seek to develop performance-based systems in higher education will soon discover that the road is not charted clearly and helpful models are scarce. But despite all the difficulties of developing performance-based systems and despite the history of partial failure in previous attempts, the necessity for educators to weigh seriously the goal of developing performance-based educational systems remains compelling. In blunt terms, higher education will use its professional expertise to develop such systems or they will very likely be developed by those who have less educational expertise and will be superimposed on present structures.

As in the planning and execution of any complex endeavor, it is necessary to develop the performance-based campus in phases. Two major starting points are advocated by those who write in the field: Begin with the top level of administration and proceed through the various levels of the campus to the courses and service areas or begin with the courses and service areas and proceed through the various levels of administration to the top of the campus. At Maimi-Dade Community College, South Campus, we chose the latter.

The project was organized into five phases. Phase 1 involved the development of measurable objectives for every course and every service area (support service) on the campus. Phase 2 involved the restatement of specific outcome objectives in simple terms and the dissemination of those statements to interested constituents such as faculty and students. Phase 3 involved the development of procedures to evaluate the degree to which students or other constituent groups achieved stated objectives. Phase 4 involved the statement of measurable objectives for every level of management on the campus. And Phase 5 involved the development of a mutual-determination system of objectives for faculty, department chairmen, division directors, campus deans, and the campus vice president—objectives that would form the basis for written performance evaluation.

The need for expertise is obvious in developing measurable objectives and evaluation systems on the part of the campus staff. The need is equally obvious for a carefully structured process in approaching the five phases. The campus approach to the development of the necessary skills began with the appointment of a Steering Committee for the Objectives Project. Through a series of workshops and much survey of the literature, the Steering Committee developed the necessary knowledge to produce guidelines and formats for the implementation of Phases 1 and 2.

Following that development, the Steering Committee members were reassigned to their departmental responsibilities and served as departmental experts, and a professional staff was appointed to head the entire effort on the campus. That staff was assigned two roles:

First, to assist faculty and administration, upon request, with acquiring the necessary technical information so that a sufficient level of sophistication could be developed which would result in the writing of objectives in measurable terms. Second, to review the work products of faculty and administrators who had been assigned responsibility for developing course and service area objectives to insure that the requirements of the published guidelines had been followed. In addition, a committee made up of the coordinator of the objectives project, the campus deans, and the campus vice president was constituted as a Campus Review Committee and charged with the responsibility of reviewing all measurable objectives for substantive and technical requirements. The review was especially valuable in delineating areas of proliferation, overlap, and duplication in the curriculum and in the support services.

To further elaborate on strategy, those who were responsible for any area of teaching or service were also responsible for producing the measurable outcome objectives for that function. The process began with courses and service areas and proceeded to the several levels of management. Finally, mutual determination of objectives, sometimes called mutual goal setting, was added as the capstone of the entire process. Apart from the commitment of the campus administration and staff to achieving defined objectives, adequate implementation of the performance-based system could not be assured. The discussion and mutual determination of objectives for faculty and administration, related to already defined objectives for courses and services, provided the incentive and the cement of the system. Without some way to tie the subsystems together into a dynamic relationship, measurable objectives and the evaluation plans were mere words on paper.

The performance-based campus offers significant benefits to those who successfully institute the concept, but attempts to develop the total system should be approached with caution. Commitment to the concept is necessary on the part of faculty and administration, a considerable degree of expertise is required, and extensive time and money must be invested. Strong educational leadership is essential at every level of administration. Progress is slow and positive results are not immediate.

For those who persist, however, significant benefits to students, faculty, and administration can be realized. Communication can be enhanced between faculty and administration, and the articulation between institutions of higher education can be improved. The efficacy of instructional and administrative strategies can be adequately tested. A feedback loop is developed upon which a self-corrective mechanism can be built. Constraints inside and outside the system are brought to the surface more rapidly. A more accurate cost-effectiveness analysis of the campus operation is possible. And educational strategy is simplified so time can be used more flexibly and creatively.

The principal strength of the performance-based campus lies in prompt identification and analysis of problems. As D. F. Walker has observed, "Education will always be in part an act of faith. But it does not have to be a leap in the dark. We can try to become aware of what we can and take the rest, hopefully a steadily diminishing range of considerations, on faith."[1] The performance-based campus can serve to diminish the scope of considerations based on faith and increase the range of those based on evidence and logic.

[1] D. F. Walker, "Educational Policy Is Flapping in the Wind," *The Center Report,* February 1974, pp. 21–25.

10

Courses by Newspaper

Caleb A. Lewis

Once a week, large and small newspapers across the country publish one in a series of 1,400-word lectures by scholars of national reputation. The papers also list the names, addresses, and phone numbers of local colleges or universities that give credit for the course of which the lecture is a part. Each participating institution provides a teacher-coordinator who conducts two contact sessions—one halfway through the series of lectures and one after the last lecture has been published. The teacher discusses the subject, answers questions, and gives home assignments. He also gives an exam and assigns grades.

The course, America and the Future of Man, was developed by University Extension, University of California, San Diego. It is the first in what is planned as a continuing series, Courses by Newspaper.

Launched by a grant from the National Endowment for the Humanities, the Courses by Newspaper program takes advantage of an existing medium—the popular press—to provide relatively inexpensive educational opportunities to millions of Americans. The newspaper lessons are distributed without charge by the Copley News Service. The first newspaper to ask from each city (or newspaper territory) receives the material. So far, 264 newspapers have accepted the first course and others continue to come in. Participating newspapers range from big-city dailies such as *The Chicago Tribune* to country weeklies. Total circulation of newspapers participating in the first course is about twenty million, with readership estimated at two or two and a half times that figure.

In an evaluation sponsored by the Exxon Education Foundation, independent survey groups called a random sample of newspaper subscribers in San Diego (*The Evening Tribune*) and Denver (*The Denver Post*). Respondents were asked whether they had read all, any, or none of the lessons. Each survey found that one in four had read one or more newspaper lessons. Extrapolated over total circulation, this would suggest a readership of at least ten million—not bad for a teacher used to reaching a few dozen students.

About one hundred eighty colleges and universities participated in the first program. Some served several papers and some served only one. Some newspapers, on the other hand, served several schools—*The Cincinnati Enquirer*, for example, had five participating colleges and universities. The number of students enrolled for credit in Courses by Newspaper was about five thousand, and about 11,500 texts and study guides have been purchased by participants.

In addition to those who take Courses by Newspaper for credit, there are two other audiences that the program seeks to serve: Those who because of handicaps, age, or unhappy early experiences in education are coming back to learning after years of being away; and those who have a continuing interest in learning (or in the subject) but no particular interest in academic credit. Many in this second group purchase the study guide and reader that accompany the course.

The second course in the series, which begins in the fall of 1974, is In Search of the American Dream. Its teacher and academic coordinator is Robert C. Elliott, professor of literature, University of California, San Diego, and a member of the Academic Advisory Committee for the first course. For course two, eighteen lectures are scheduled (a semester-oriented number) instead of the original twenty. Once again participation is wide open, and those newspapers and institutions that participated the first time around have been invited to continue the relationship.

The evaluation of the first course was not completed at the time this article was written. If the evaluation is favorable, Courses by Newspaper might encourage the development of other national educational programs to serve heretofore unreachable learners. The benefit of such efforts is that virtually everyone, rather than just a privileged few, can have access to the nation's best teacher-scholars. Through the first course, millions of Americans took part in "classes" taught by professors from Harvard, Stanford, Michigan, Cal Tech, the London School of Economics, Yale, St. John's College, and other renowned institutions.

Newspapers are just one way of providing national access; there are others. One program, in fact, has linked up with University Extension, University of California, San Diego, to develop an audio-cassette counterpart to Courses by Newspaper. This program, administered by the Center for Cassette Studies in North Hollywood, has been using libraries to distribute audio cassettes of great teachers from coast to coast. The cassettes are issued like books, and all you need to check one out is a library card. They are marketed to libraries by Xerox and are accompanied by a machine that dubs copies quickly, so that no matter how many people want a particular tape, they can get it. The library patron may also dub the cassette at home for his own personal library. University Extension is preparing five experimental national credit courses for the Center and expects to have them ready by the fall of 1975. Study guides, readers, and a teacher's manual will accompany the cassettes.

National programs through newspapers, library cassettes, or other means provide an unparalleled opportunity to reach large numbers of people with top-quality instructional material. The programs are possible because of economic wide distribution and because the means for presenting them (newspapers, libraries) already exist. Instruction per student costs only a fraction of more traditional learning structures. At University of California Extension, San Diego, for example, we can seldom afford to bring in a national figure from the East Coast to guest lecture. The air fare alone makes it impractical. But with three to seven campuses sharing the fare, we found we were able to have more talent more often. If a small group of campuses can afford better speakers by pooling travel money, think what a national program can do.

It might be argued that such a scheme will aggravate an already declining market for teachers since one professor, instead of reaching twenty or a hundred students with a lecture, can reach millions. The same argument surfaced when the first videotaped credit courses came out. The market for teachers didn't collapse then and it's not likely to do so now. The market for courses and teachers is expanding rapidly. People live longer and retire earlier. National programming will expand the learning market further by turning on those who were turned off, by reaching those who have not been reached, and by developing better, more exciting, and more accessible instructional programs.

The future of national programming is unlimited, and it has only begun to be explored. To my knowledge, only two programs have actually been mounted: "Sunrise Semester" on TV and Courses by Newspaper. I think we're going to have a lot more.

11

Cooperative
Approach

George P. Connick

Ｍaine has a population of only a little over one million people in an area as large as the other five New England states combined. The state has some of the most diverse and strikingly beautiful scenery in the country and four distinct seasons, highlighted by warm summers and cold snowy winters. The average family income ranks 37th in the nation.

In terms of postsecondary education, Maine ranks last in the nation in the percent of high-school seniors who continue their schooling (45 percent). Maine has a university system with eight campuses consisting of two university centers, four state colleges, and two community colleges; the system has a total enrollment of twenty-five thousand students. There are six vocational-technical centers directed by the State Department of Education, with a combined enrollment of 2,500, and there are nineteen proprietary schools and fifteen private colleges. Six of Maine's sixteen counties have a university campus, six have a vocational-technical institute, and ten counties have neither.

The most southerly county is York, with a population of 106,000 and no public postsecondary institution. The York County town of Sanford, population sixteen thousand, is a typical Maine town. Sanford has twelve churches, thirteen bars, twelve restaurants, an active adult education program, a public library with seventy-two thousand volumes, and a small hospital. Sanford has one private liberal-arts college, Nasson, with approximately nine hundred students. The public postsecondary institutions closest to Sanford—the University of Maine at Portland-Gorham and Southern Maine Vocational-Technical Institute—are forty miles away. Sanford, like the great majority of small communities in Maine, has insufficient population to justify the state investing in the construction of a community college or other type of postsecondary institution. Yet there are certainly enough people of all ages who want and need postsecondary opportunities to warrant the state providing them in some way.

Faculty and administrators in higher education are undergoing, often reluctantly, a gradual transformation of their views about higher education and of the role their own institution plays in that transformation. New life styles and changing student career preferences, new priorities for public and private dollars, and the resulting contraction of educational budgets have forced us to reassess what we are about. And what we are about, of course, is a transition, even though we may disagree on where we have been, where we want to go, and the details for getting there. Harry Truman once said that "getting people to do something often requires flattering, kissing, and kicking them to do the things they should have done in the first place." Maine, like other states, has been attempting to deal with both the theory of transition and the process for achieving it—the flattering, kissing, and kicking.

In the past eight years, ten major studies dealing with postsecondary education in Maine have urged that educational access be expanded to the largely bypassed portion of the state's population. Confronted in the late 1960s and early 1970s with the same financial difficulties plaguing other states, Maine found it difficult to implement more than a handful of the recommendations in these studies. Believing that educational expansion needed to be carefully coordinated in the future, the chancellor of the University of Maine and the commissioner of education, in December 1972, invited the presidents of the four private colleges in southern Maine to discuss how education not leading to a baccalaureate might be extended to more people. A planning committee was formed, headed by the director of academic planning and two faculty members from the University of Maine at Portland-Gorham, with representatives from Southern Maine Vocational-Technical Institute, and four private colleges—Westbrook, St. Francis, St. Joseph's and Nasson.

After careful study, the committee identified four problems as being paramount in restricting access to postsecondary education in Maine. First, the existing fourteen public and fifteen private colleges are primarily baccalaureate-granting institutions although the job opportunities in Maine tend to be eight times greater for associate-degree graduates. Second, the state cannot afford to construct and maintain additional campuses, especially in sparsely populated sections of the state. Third, a sizable number of Maine citizens of all ages live too far from the existing campuses to make commuting realistic during the severe Maine winters. And fourth, those citizens living beyond commuting distance tend to have the lowest family incomes, and because of the expense for resident students are least likely to send their children away to school or attend themselves.

The committee's final plan offered solutions to these four problems. First, a community college structure was proposed that would offer comprehensive occupational, technical, and liberal-arts programs, and other services to meet the economic and cultural needs of each region. Second, the plan provided that rather than construct new buildings, the state should utilize existing public and private educational institutions and facilities such as public libraries, armories, museums, historical societies, community centers, and hospitals. A third recommendation was that the heart of the community college in each locale should be a counseling center, using leased facilities near the downtown area to make it convenient and inexpensive for people to take advantage of the services.

On July 5, 1973, the plan was approved by the chancellor of the University of Maine; the commissioner of educational and cultural services, who is responsible for the vocational-technical institutes; and the four private college presidents. On July 5, 1973, the decision was made to test the model in York, the oldest of the sixteen counties in Maine.

York County, known as the "Gateway to Maine," is wonderfully picturesque and rich with historic landmarks—forts, lighthouses, museums, and fine old homes. York is the ninth largest county in Maine, encompassing an area of one thousand square miles. It ranks third in population and is the fastest growing area in the state. York was the only county in Maine in which all cities or towns registered population increases from 1960 to 1970. The coastal towns of the area have relatively small year-round populations, but during the summer months the people who seek to escape the noise, dirt, and confusion of city life often increase the numbers fivefold to tenfold.

Life in York County is difficult for many families. The Bureau of Labor Statistics of the U.S. Department of Labor estimates that a family of four needed an income in 1970 of about $11,230 to have an intermediate standard of living in southern Maine. This budget provided enough to maintain health and well being and allowed a degree of discretionary spending on food, housing, and clothes. But it allowed a mere $690 per year for such items as gifts, contributions, entertainment, *and* education. In York County, 71 percent of the families have incomes below this standard. Furthermore, York is the state's most heavily populated county without a publicly supported postsecondary institution although it has two private colleges, St. Francis and Nasson.

York was chosen as the ideal place to test the model for several reasons. The low-income level of its residents restricted access to postsecondary education, the county lacked any public postsecondary institution, and the two private colleges were located in the largest towns in the county—Biddeford and Sanford. These towns were willing to lease facilities and services for late afternoon and evening classes, and because St. Francis and Nasson are twenty miles apart in the center of York County, over 60 percent of the population would be within ten miles of one of these new community learning centers.

This new model, named York County Community College Services, is a unique institution. To date, seven educational institutions are involved in the project. The University of Maine at Portland-Gorham and the University of Maine at Augusta have extended their programs in liberal arts, general studies, and business administration to York County, and Southern Maine Vocational-Technical Institute has extended programs in building construction, emergency medical technology, and law enforcement. In addition, the University of Maine at Portland-Gorham and Southern Maine Vocational-Technical Institute have developed a joint Hotel-Motel-Restaurant Management program which is being offered through York County Community College Services. Space for classes has been provided by the Sanford and Biddeford public schools, and through lease arrangements Nasson and St. Francis colleges have provided classrooms, laboratories, faculty offices, and essential library and bookstore support.

Within eight weeks of the July 5 meeting, a host of administrative details were completed. These included hiring counseling staff and faculty, opening counseling offices, releasing publicity, and the negotiation of leases. York County Community College Services began classes on September 5 with thirty-eight courses and 315 students. Now, in the second semester, enrollment is nearly double that of the fall and at a cost to the state significantly lower than that of the existing publicly supported campuses. Of greatest significance, perhaps, are the student-survey results which indicate that almost 90 percent of the students are attending college for the first time and that they would not be attending at all if it had not been made available close to home at low cost.

Now that the initial aspect of the model has been successfully launched, the second phase is being planned. An instructional system still in the development stage will be open-entry, open-exit. The system will utilize diagnostic methods to assist in prescribing individualized learning sequences and will allow students to work at their own pace on a competency-based curriculum. The use of instructional technology —films, audio and video tapes, slides, and computers—is expected to reduce the cost of instruction further when the model is expanded to accommodate large numbers of students.

The model being tested in York County has shown that comprehensive postsecondary education can be provided for citizens in a variety of degree programs, within a reasonable commuting distance, at relatively low cost for the individual and the state, and without construction of new buildings or campuses. The model owes its success to the cooperative efforts of a number of institutions. The original goal of this project was to demonstrate that postsecondary education could be provided to those citizens, who, for whatever reasons, were unable to take advantage of the existing educational system. Although still new, the York County model appears to be working. And what works in York County may work elsewhere in Maine. Or any other state, for that matter.

12

Open University in America

Betty Jo Mayeske

The Open University of the United Kingdom was chartered by the Queen on May 30, 1969, as an independent autonomous university with power to award its own degrees. Sometimes referred to as the *University of the Second Chance,* it was directed to make available to persons over twenty-one academic opportunities at the college level. In the 1960s in the UK, less than 10 percent of the age group between eighteen and twenty could attend conventional universities. Thus a need was recognized, and government funds were allotted to cover 85 percent of the costs while the remaining 15 percent would come from student fees.

The new university was charged with the responsibility of structuring educational approaches that considered the life style of active adults who would have to study on a part-time basis. Further, the OU was to make full use of the educational potential of BBC TV and radio. And the university was to maintain traditional academic values and re-emphasize the concept of interdisciplinary studies and the general degree. The campus of the Open University is located in Milton Keynes, fifty miles northwest of London. Here there is office space for the teaching and administrative staff, a library, laboratories, special buildings for the publication of academic material, and, soon to be completed, operations for the production of television material.

Six credits are necessary to obtain an Open University BA degree. Each credit represents about thirty-six weeks of work. Academic course teams, working in conjunction with BBC producers, prepared interdisciplinary foundation courses in humanities, social science, natural science, technology, and mathematics. For a degree, the student must take two foundation courses and four upper-level courses at one credit each to total six credits. Presently there are sixty-eight completed courses with twelve new ones planned for completion yearly.

The teaching system includes correspondence texts geared for independent study. These student-active texts allow the student to pause, reflect, agree or disagree, and give feedback. Set books—texts dealing with specialized topics—accompany the correspondence units. A twenty-five-minute TV production for the weekly work supplements the foundation-level course assignments with dramatic documentaries, discussion, or laboratory experiments. Twenty-five-minute weekly radio programs often carry interviews with eminent guest speakers or group discussions by academic authorities.

Because this independent study system could allow the student to feel too isolated and to fall behind, the OU made personal contact an integral part of the system. Tutors and counselors are available to the student by mail, phone, or at learning centers. These specially trained people are able to provide the type of attention and guidance determined by the needs and the schedules of the students. Two hundred seventy learning centers are located throughout the UK. Here students and tutors meet, discuss, argue, listen, and go over the weekly material. Attendance at a week-long summer session for the foundation courses allows students to review, attend supplementary lectures, discuss material, and work in fully equipped science labs. Students must attend this summer session, submit assignments throughout the year, and sit for a proctored final exam. The OU currently enrolls over thirty-seven thousand students in its sixty-eight courses. Over 4,500 have graduated, 170 of whom had no previous university training.

To many Americans, the OU of the UK was an exciting educational endeavor, implemented at great financial cost (the average cost of a foundation course is about $1 million). In an effort to discover whether the materials and the learning system could be used by American institutions, the Carnegie Foundation funded a study by the Educational Testing Service under the direction of Hartnett to report on the use of the OU course materials at three American Institutions: the University of Houston, Rutgers, and the University of Maryland.[1] The material that follows was drawn largely from that report, which was available only in manuscript form at the time of this writing.

All three universities had been in the process of examining individual OU courses with respect to their own degree structure. In September, 1972, Rutgers offered humanities, natural science, and the mathematics foundation courses for fifteen (U.S.) credits each; enrollment for the entire course cost $300. The University of Houston offered humanities for twelve credits and science for fourteen credits, each divided into two equal semesters. The cost was $50 for humanities and $56 for science. At University College, University of Maryland, humanities was offered for eighteen credits in three, six-credit terms. Tuition cost for the entire course was $450. University College is one of five campuses at the University of Maryland. For twenty-five years, it has been involved in adult continuing education, and in 1974 enrolled over twenty-four thousand students in the Washington-Baltimore area and overseas.

The immediate concern of all three universities was to find qualified students interested in such a learning experience. Rutgers enrolled 228, with no formal academic requirements. Houston enrolled 109 regularly admitted undergraduates. At University College, 304 adults with a high-school diploma were enrolled on a first-come, first-served basis. My own survey of first-year students at the University College OU shows that the average age of the students is thirty-five years; 63 percent are female, 37 percent male; 17 percent are members of minority groups; 25 percent had no previous college, while 40

[1] Rodney Hartnett, *The British Open University in the United States: Adaptation and Use at Three Universities* (Princeton: Educational Testing Service, 1974).

percent had not been to school for seven to ten years; 52.63 percent are employed full-time, 9.21 percent part-time, and 22.3 percent are housewives.

Learning systems varied among the three American universities. Rutgers had two study centers for humanities; Houston had one classroom seminar with separate tutorial headquarters; and Maryland had thirteen learning centers throughout the Washington-Baltimore area in public libraries, high schools, and military installations. All three universities staffed the centers with graduate assistants and faculty members. Houston showed films on closed-circuit campus TV. At Maryland, all tutors carried 16 mm projectors to the centers. Maryland alone presented the obligatory on-campus seminar. This six-day experience was divided into three weekends, held near the end of each term. The first weekend session included taking all three hundred students to the National Gallery of Art in Washington, D.C., and scheduling speeches by guest professors.

Results of the year in brief show that 48 percent of the students at Rutgers completed the thirty-six week humanities course, 52 percent finished at Houston, and 50 percent at Maryland. The students provided much data on their experiences, attitudes, and reactions to the courses and the learning system. It was found that participation in the OU courses was time-consuming for students. Over half reported spending more than twelve hours per week on the material, yet many spent more than sixteen hours on their assignments. The major source of dissatisfaction among those who completed the entire course was the logistical difficulty of finding time to do the required work. Student criticism of the British-oriented OU materials was minimal. Though the OU is often referred to as an independent study program, students regarded contact with both tutors and other OU students as important for grasping the concepts of the course content. Because of their positive experience, nearly half of the humanities students reported that they were much more interested in pursuing a college degree and had more confidence in their ability to do college-level work.

As the result of a successful experimental year, University College of the University of Maryland continued the Open University courses it had been offering and added new ones. In the fall of its second year, 1973, the Open University Division offered the humanities foundation course, which includes history, literature, art, music, religion, and philosophy. The division introduced the social-science foundation course, which presents sociology, psychology, economics, political science, and geography; the technology foundation course, which demonstrates the social and environmental impact of technologies and discusses the work of environmental technologists, systems analysts, and engineers; the mathematics foundation course, which integrates logic, probability, statistics, calculus, linear algebra, and complex numbers; and the natural-science foundation course, which includes physics, chemistry, biology, and geology. For persons who had completed the humanities foundation course or who held junior standing, the OU second-level course—the renaissance and reformation—was offered. This course presents a thorough look at the history, literature, art, music, philosophy, and religion of Europe from 1300 to 1600.

All the courses added by University College in its second year award eighteen credits and are delivered in three terms. Students are currently served by thirty-one learning centers in the Washington-Baltimore area. Adaptation was necessary with the social-science course but could be achieved by keeping the OU correspondence texts, films, and tapes, and changing the obligatory readings. With respect to laboratory equipment designed for the academic needs of the course, University College imported from England the necessary academic kits, which cost $300 each, and lent them to all students in the natural-science program. Included in the kit is a microscope, a balance, a colorimeter, and a variety of chemicals and laboratory glassware. In a further effort to approximate more completely the OU teaching system, the films supporting technology and humanities are run on educational and public TV (WETA and MPBS). To air these films publicly, University College pays copyright fees to the Open University of the UK.

The multidisciplinary nature of the OU courses has presented a staffing challenge. Tutors are hired on the basis of their academic background and college teaching experience. They are asked to ignore their formal lecture background and serve as resource persons. Since one tutor stays with a student throughout the entire course—meeting him at the center, conducting phone tutorials, grading assignments and final exams—tutors have had to gain academic background in several disciplines. The formation of a staff acquainted with interdisciplinary material has been accomplished by weekly staff-tutor meetings. Films and tapes are previewed, academic expertise is shared, and effective tutorial methods are discussed. The system works and works well.

Many of the 404 students currently enrolled in OU courses at Maryland have requested further OU courses. University College plans to add second-level courses in all five faculties and to reoffer all five foundation-level courses. The college will call on a variety of departments to examine the courses with respect to the existing Maryland degree structure. The Open University courses and teaching system have demonstrated an important and flexible alternative for the active adult pursuing a University of Maryland degree.

PART THREE

On the Horizon

The authors of Part Three go one step further than new programs. They speculate about future arrangements that could transform the idea of a learning society into reality. These educators offer proposals for new national systems and report on projects still in the germinal stage. In some instances—for example, Morris Keeton's recommendations on learning networks—what is called for is a reshaping of existing resources and relationships to increase the quality and quantity of learning without substantially increasing costs. In others—such as the proposals by Nancy Schlossberg and Robin Wilson—new systems would have to emerge, but the resulting increase in services would mean greater cost efficiency and better use of human resources in the long run.

What Schlossberg and Wilson call for is a nationwide system of learning "brokers" to match people with the learning resources that can best meet their needs—educationally, financially, geographically, and otherwise. Learning brokers, whom Wilson sees as working for learners the way travel agencies work for travelers, encapsulates the whole idea of making learning a service Americans can use throughout their lives. The chapter points up the need to identify the vast national complex of learning resources so that learners can find out what and where these resources are, and Wilson indicates the kind of national effort needed to bring about a more efficient system of learning. The resources are there. The demand for them is there. What is lacking, it seems, is the delivery systems that can bring the two together.

Interestingly, the chapters in this section are not alternative proposals for a learning society. The proposals are remarkably compatible, even down to the terminology. The idea of an "educational passport" described by John Summerskill and John Osander, for example, fits beautifully with Wilson's travel-agency analogy. The passport, a proposed document that would serve as a handy portable record of a student's educational experience, "would be the student's personal property, and the student would use it to move from high school to college, from college to college, from school to job, from job to school, and so on." The fact is, learners move around. The educational passport recognizes and seeks to accommodate this mobility.

Approaching the subject of credentialing from another angle, Harold L. Hodgkinson contends that it may be time for higher education to get out of that aspect altogether. Hodgkinson proposes "that two systems of awards be developed—the first dealing entirely with degrees as statements of intellectual interest and experience, and the second dealing with credentials that are based on proficiency and are job related and job predictive." The degree would be handled by educational institutions. The credentialing would be handled by regional examining institutes and would be concerned with determining what people know and can do rather than with how much formal education they have had. To institutions struggling with attracting students, giving up credentialing powers may seem like throwing away three aces to try drawing a straight. But Hodgkinson, like the other authors of Part Two, is not looking at the issue from the view of institutional interest so much as from the view of students and the society.

K. Patricia Cross, who writes the lead chapter in the section, is less concerned with systems to expedite learning or extend it to more people than with reforming the process itself. The present system, she argues, does not educate the whole person, but only the head. People who are good at working with ideas do well scholastically, but what of people who are good at working with their hands or who are good at working with other people? What Cross proposes is a three-dimensional system that would not only allow people to succeed in areas where they have the most talent, but would help all students develop at least minimum competence in their weakest areas.

Part Two showed the first steps toward a learning society. The authors of Part Three offer thoughtful advice on how to go the rest of the way.

WILLIAM FERRIS

13

New Forms for
New Functions

K. Patricia Cross

Without much advance planning and without even articulating the change very explicitly, higher education has recently accepted a function quite different from what it performed in the 1940s and 1950s. The difference between educating only those that we have selected and educating everyone who walks through the open door is profound, and it is a change that is having an impact on all colleges—selective as well as open-door institutions.

In the heyday of selective admissions, prestige automatically accompanied selectivity. The best colleges were those that selected freshmen who already had most of the characteristics desired for seniors. Education was perceived as a low-risk venture where you got out about what you put in, and the reputation of the college was as likely to be established by the admissions office as by the faculty. Today we expect more of education. We are now trying to evaluate colleges on the basis of their skill in educating students rather than for their skill in selecting students. People are beginning to talk about "value added" and about the processes of teaching and learning. Even that quaint old-fashioned word, *pedagogy,* is making a comeback. The task of education, as we see it now, is not to select those who will be successful but to make successful those who come.

When we compare the functions of higher education in the 1950s with those of today, it seems as though the 1950s were cursed with a generation of misguided pragmatists possessing limited vision for higher education. But then, as now, the task of educational institutions was to develop the talent pool that is needed by the collective society. And, then as now, people were doing their best to meet those needs. The academic meritocracy reached its peak during the years of the cold war. The perceived need was for an intellectual leadership that could compete with that of Russia and assure national growth and progress. Our societal needs today are dramatically different. Production and growth are not as important as conservation and learning to live in the steady state. Discovery and technological advance are not as important as human development and social reform—as witness the national indifference to the re-entry of the astronauts and the rising interest in health programs.

Somewhat to our chagrin, we in education are discovering that Detroit is not the only establishment having trouble adjusting to the new needs of society. If you are tooled up for Cadillacs and your staff knows how to make quality Cadillacs, it is hard to believe that Volkswagens and Toyotas may really be superior models for the changing world. Colleges and faculty that won their prestige with an all-out push for academic excellence in the 1950s find it difficult indeed to tool up for new models. The position that is staunchly defended by most faculty members is that while it is quite all right to admit a diversity of talent to colleges, academic standards must be preserved and no one should be graduated without meeting those standards. It is as though we put a Volkswagen on the assembly line, added a heavy motor, extended the hood, enlarged the trunk, put in expensive carpets and interiors, and insisted on the smooth ride of a heavy car—all in the interest of maintaining standards. A Volkswagen is not a cheaper, lighter Cadillac; it is a different car designed for different purposes. Similarly, college for the masses is not a low-standard version of college for the elite; it is a different kind of education with high standards true to its own purposes.

What kind of standards do we need for our new purposes? It is difficult to grasp the enormity of the impact that societal change is having on education. Consider, for example, a basic problem—the fact that the task of conveying information in the academic disciplines is becoming untenable as a teaching function. The knowledge explosion is now a fact of life. Every forty minutes enough new information is generated to fill a twenty-four volume encyclopedia. Anyone who regards academic information as the backbone of education might do well to ponder an epigram that is a favorite with medical students, "A general practitioner learns less and less about more and more, until he eventually knows nothing about everything, while the specialist learns more and more about less and less until he eventually knows everything about nothing."

A second problem presented by our present model of education is that the academic disciplines form too narrow a base on which to build a society. We already know that academic success is not highly related to success in life outside of academe, however one chooses to define *success*. It is possible that we have overemphasized the importance of that narrow range of human abilities that enable people to perform academic tasks in the school system. We are now told that only 20 percent of the jobs during the 1980s will utilize knowledge learned by a college student. There is no doubt that society will always need to nurture and develop intellectual competence of the highest order. But when we attempt to cast everyone in the same mold, we sell short both society and individual human beings. It may be time for some new models of education—that are true to the integrity of individuals as well as to the needs of society.

In what follows, I would like to present a model that emphasizes high standards, to be sure, but that meets the needs of the new clientele and the new society as well.

The new clientele of higher education is a more diverse group of students than any in the previous history of higher education. Open access to college must mean more than opening a broad funnel to admit diversity and then narrowing the neck so that only the preferred pass through. We need to expand the concept of academic excellence and to speak in broader terms of educational excellence. The most disturbing data that I had to deal with in my research on new students was that students who had not done well in school learned to think of themselves as below-average people. School is geared to the development of a narrow range of talent consisting of approximately one-twelfth of the known human abilities; it is not surprising that students whose chief talents lie among the unexploited eleven-twelfths have trouble demonstrating that they can make contributions to society.

It is a statistical fact that on any single dimension of human ability, half the students in the nation will be below average by definition. Naive egalitarians have the notion that working with the bottom half will somehow raise them to equal status with the top half. Unfortunately, status in the society is relative, and on any single measure there will always be a lower half. There is, however, a way to reduce the number in the lower half, and that is to expand the number of dimensions along which talent is measured. If talent is measured on two independent dimensions, then 75 percent will be above average on one or the other dimension. If three independent talents are assumed, the statistical probability is that 87.5 percent will be above average on one of the three dimensions. Human abilities tend to be modestly related; a relationship exists between high-school grades and leadership positions. This modest correlation, however, may be attributed more to the success experiences and the resultant self-confidence of the good student than it may be to any innate relationship between academic and social abilities.

We know that there are individual differences in academic ability and that those differences are unrelated to the color of one's skin, height, weight, or any other physical characteristic. Exactly how much of what we call academic aptitude is due to environment and how much to heredity is a question that defies our methodology at present. But the issue is important only if we assume that people with high academic ability are worth more than those with talents in other areas. If we persist in thinking that the ability to perform academic tasks is a measure of human worth, then we face the prospect of creating a new group of "disadvantaged" that consists not necessarily of minority groups or poor people but of all those from any strata of society with below-average academic aptitude. While we believe that people should not be relegated to second-class citizenship on the basis of skin color or sex, social institutions may still be relegating certain groups—in this case those with low academic interests and abilities—to lower status in the society.

Jerome Kagan of Harvard goes so far as to say that he wants "children rank-ordered on the basis of humanism as we rank-order on the basis of reading and mathematics." He claims that schools exist to serve the needs of society and that the greatest need now is to restore faith, honesty, and humanity. He says, "I am suggesting in deep seriousness that we must, in the school, begin to reward those traits as the Spartans rewarded physical fitness."[1] While I agree with Kagan that we must reward the characteristics that are valued by society, I don't think we make progress by replacing one unidimensional system with another—although perhaps we all have more equal opportunity to be good humanitarians than we have to be good academicians.

We might begin gearing education to the needs of society by matching the cultivation of individual talents to societal needs in a three-dimensional model patterned after the skills needed in occupations as they are defined in the *Dictionary of Occupational Titles,* published by the United States Employment Service. USES has determined that work can be described by three major functions—work with data, work with people, and work with things. Most jobs consist of combinations of the three functions and are classified in the dictionary according to the level of skill required in each area.

I propose that the task of education is to develop the student's greatest talent in these three areas to the point of excellence, and that we also prepare him for his environment by developing at least minimum competence in the other two areas. Students would have the option of selecting the area or areas in which to pursue excellence. The student who has interest and ability in the manipulation of ideas would pursue academic excellence, but he would also be required to develop minimum levels of competence in working with things and people. Future sculptors or auto mechanics would pursue excellence in the manipulation of tools and materials, but also would develop basic competence in traditional academic subjects and in working with people. The development of interpersonal skills would no longer be left to extracurricular activities and to chance but would be consciously developed so that future counselors, receptionists, and social workers could pursue excellence in human relations. No skill would be considered better or higher than any other; all are equally important to our society.

The advantage of this program in our egalitarian future is that it recognizes individual differences and gives more people an opportunity to make real and valued contributions. The educational ad-

[1] "Do the First Two Years Matter? A Conversation with Jerome Kagan," *Saturday Review—Education,* April, 1973, *1*(3), p. 41.

vantage of the proposal is that it permits us to establish realistic standards of performance. The best we can do at present, given our elitist form of higher education and our egalitarian function, is to be tolerant of those who cannot meet academic standards. Proposals to abolish grading are an example of this tolerance. If we must rate people for unidimensional talent, the abolition of grading is the only way to avoid the stigma of failure for the lower half.

My proposed reform of education casts a new light on remedial education. All of us have weaknesses, not just the so-called disadvantaged, and all of us need remediation. Consider, for example, the academically oriented doctor's son who is elected president of the student body but who is totally dependent on others to tell him how things work. He is disadvantaged when it comes to working with things, and he has many of the symptoms of the academically disadvantaged. The boy's father knows nothing about mechanics and lacks even a basic vocabulary to help his son learn. Just as there are few good books in the homes of the educationally disadvantaged, so there are few good tools in the homes of the mechanically disadvantaged. I do not propose that remediation for this high-risk mechanic should consist of learning to fix his own car if he has no interest or talent in that direction. But I do suggest that he should be exposed to some remediation in basic learning about how things work. I know college professors whose total dependence on others to tell them what goes on under the hood of their car is just as sad as the failure of the poorly educated to understand the cost of buying on credit. Neither is equipped to make informed decisions about important realities of their lives.

Nothing would be more salutary, I think, than to develop the kind of learning society in which the able academician but poor mechanic exchanges tutoring services with the slow reader but good mechanic. Each would be teaching in his area of excellence and learning in his area of proposed competence.

All that is necessary to implement this model for educational diversity is that we ask each student to select his area of excellence with the understanding that tough standards will be imposed. He can start anywhere he chooses; remediation will be provided in all three areas. A student deficient in academic skills may still elect this area of excellence, but with the understanding that it may take longer to get his degree and that he will have to meet the same standards as others pursuing academic excellence. Grades, honors, tests, and all the other trappings used to measure performance in the academy will be applied to the area of excellence. Such measures, of course, will be appropriate to the skill being evaluated. Written tests may be appropriate in evaluating knowledge skills, for example, whereas one might use oral tests for interpersonal skills and performance tests for those seeking excellence in working with things. In the area of competence, however, there will be no grades except pass. Either the student is certified as meeting minimum standards of competence or he takes remediation until he is.

I am making my proposal very specific, not because I wish to defend this particular model as solving all our problems, but because I hope to get educators to stand back and take a fresh look at some of the assumptions that we have made into eternal verities. Equal opportunity means more than the opportunity to develop mediocre competence in the area of someone else's strength. Equal opportunity means being provided with the tools to develop one's own talents to the point of excellence. Most people today speak of education for diversity as though it were education by diversity. We are willing to entertain the idea that people can learn the same things by different methods or in differing amounts of time—although we are slow to implement even those obvious facts. When we do implement them, it is with the implicit understanding that some students will take to traditional academic learning like a duck to water, while others will struggle to remain afloat. Never mind that our sinking duck can run like a gazelle or fly like a swallow. What we are not yet ready to concede is that running or flying is as good as swimming and that our world is better for the existence of all three abilities, appropriately used.

14

Educational
Passport

John Summerskill, John Osander

The educational passport is proposed as a document that would contain a student's credentials from the educational world. The passport would be the student's personal property, and the student would use it to move from high school to college, from college to college, from school to job, from job to school, and so on. The concept of the passport is being developed by Educational Testing Service. Field trials are scheduled for 1974–1975.[1]

The genesis of the idea lies in the changing nature of postsecondary education, the changes taking place in the population participating in postsecondary education, and the impact on the processes of

[1] After this article was written, development of the educational passport was funded by a grant of $100,000 from the Lilly Endowment.

93

entry and re-entry into the educational system. It is doubtful that ETS would be proposing the development of something called an *educational passport* if we were still in an era when going to college meant just a one-time movement from four years of secondary school to four years of college. But the pursuit of education beyond secondary school today means many different things to many different people. There are approximately 3.3 million high-school graduates each year. Approximately one-third of these go directly to four-year colleges, approximately 11 percent go to two-year academic colleges, and 5 percent to two-year technical colleges. Thus half of the high-school graduates start to college although less than half of these graduate from their initial colleges "on schedule." The other half of the high-school graduating class goes in different directions, with perhaps 50 percent entering jobs directly. Of the remainder, some 9 percent go to vocational-technical schools, and smaller percentages enter apprenticeships and the military services where their formal education is continued.

To make the statistics more complex, students simply won't stay in their educational categories any more. Perfectly good college students quit and go to work and perfectly good workers quit and go to college. Students from community colleges transfer into four-year colleges while graduates of four-year colleges take postgraduate work at community colleges. Mature women rush back to college for courses in the psychology and sociology of male dominance as their spouses seek formal instruction in modern techniques of housewifery and midwifery. In the midst of this academic chaos and scholarly disorder, an idea as simple as the educational passport just might help.

The passport itself is nothing but a single 4" × 6" microcard in an appropriate envelope or folder. This microcard is durable, inexpensive, and easily read and copied. On the sheet of microcard, in photographically reduced form, are all the records of educational progress that one might want to keep and present—high-school grades, recommendations from teachers, scores, college grades, instructors' comments, narrative testimonies, summaries of special projects or special training, outcomes of experiential learning, personal statements of accomplishment, and so on. The student can include in the passport what he chooses and, indeed, a student can construct his own passport if he chooses.

In practice, regional and national educational agencies that have the appropriate personnel and equipment will, in all likelihood, prepare passports for students and keep them up to date at the request of students. When a student wants to enroll in an educational program, he will simply present his passport to the educational institution, where credentials can be reviewed on the spot using an inexpensive microfiche viewer. An index will help the institution find categories of information in the passport that are of special interest. If the institution wants a basic permanent record for the student who is admitted (or employed), this can be supplied, at the student's request, by the agency that issued the passport.

As for the problems and issues surrounding the concept of the educational passport, these are divided into four areas: ethical considerations, policy and organization, procedural and technical considerations, and the economics of the educational passport system.

With regard to ethics, the individual must determine and control whatever material is contained in the passport. The learner must decide how and when the passport is updated, when and to whom it is issued. In addition, because decisions are made from passports that affect the lives and careers of individuals and the integrity of institutions, the authenticity of the documents must be guaranteed.

Problems of policy and organization are, perhaps, even thornier. Registrars of individual colleges and universities have traditionally taken prime responsibility for recording and transcripting student credentials, but should they or some other agency run the passport system in behalf of students? Will local and regional passport agencies be more convenient and effective, or will national passport systems be necessary to serve a mobile, adult, student population? And if students send records, or have records sent, to regional or national passport agencies, what will be the political, procedural, and financial arrangements with the teaching institutions? There are plenty of additional questions in this category, and they will have to be answered before a comprehensive system can be established.

As for procedural and technical aspects, we must evaluate and select systems and equipment that work easily and efficiently. We must develop passport indexing, procedures for passport agencies, time requirements, updating cycles, and more. These are problems for which solutions exist, but much effort will be needed to match processes with the right mechanisms.

Finally, the financial viability of the educational passport is still to be determined, although the concept has encountered, through informal channels, considerable student interest. Specifically, there will have to be further analysis of the actual need and demand for passports, cost estimating for alternative systems models, and projections of fee structures that would permit a break-even operation.

So there is still much work to be done before educational passports can become a reality. But hopefully it is work that will enhance the progress of those pursuing their education in different ways, at different times. In addition to simplifying the admissions process for all concerned, the passport can reflect a student's achievement in broader terms than grades and test scores alone. The passport is really a composite biography and should reduce tension between those who view education as mere credentialing and those interested in the learning experience as such. Further, the passport will permit the recording of learning experiences on the job, in the community, overseas—learning experiences which the typical academic transcript does not easily accommodate. Thus, the passport will assist in evaluating an individual's overall progress in attaining his educational goals and will help in planning the next steps.

If implemented on a national scale, the educational passport should enhance access to postsecondary education for countless individuals. The passport should promote more meaningful and flexible learning experiences by broadening evaluation beyond letter grades and scores, and it should increase the effectiveness of educational counseling and planning.

15

Regional Examining Institutes

Harold L. Hodgkinson

Access to the credentialing process is still largely contingent on the amount of higher education, or its equivalent, to which one has been exposed. Those who cannot give up other responsibilities for an extended period of higher education often have a difficult time fulfilling their job aspirations. The problem is particularly difficult for people who would like to move into a second career. The nurse who wishes to use her education credits toward becoming a doctor is usually advised that she will have to "go back to zero" before beginning advanced work. Similarly, a person with a degree in social work who wishes to enter a law school may find it impossible to get credit toward a law degree for the competence he possesses in certain aspects of law.

It seems important that the credentialing process consider what candidates actually know and can do rather than insist that certain educational exposures be completed before the credentialing process can even begin. The B.A. degree is considered an absolute necessity today for entering professional study, even though there is little evidence that the degree is a necessity for success in advanced professional work. Indeed, it seems that credentialism and teaching often work against each other. The student wishing to enter medical school is told that a broad general education is necessary to be a good physician, yet premed undergraduate days are often spent in preparing for the Medical College Admission Tests. As a result, the premed student seldom gets a good general education at the B.A. level, not even in science. This suggests that the functions of teaching and credentialing be kept separate, handled by different people with different skills in different agencies. Some people can be credentialed without teaching and others may just wish to be taught and not credentialed.

A related line of argument is that there needs to be a fairly sharp distinction between the awarding of credentials and the awarding of college degrees. Viewed in this way, a college degree would be primarily an award based on required years of academic study and would indicate a student's areas of intellectual interest, skill, and commitment. The degree, particularly the baccalaureate, would have little or no use in job-related credentialing. The job-related system of credentialing would be removed from the complete control of higher-education institutions and would be handled by a variety of groups. These could include successful practitioners of a particular occupation, clients, members of regulatory agencies, and professional examiners as well as faculty members. The credential then becomes a direct prediction of occupational success for a given area of work and that alone. A number of studies support this position; they have indicated little relationship between the criteria for success in higher education (grades) and the criteria applied in the outside world.

In place of the inadequate and inaccurate single-system approach, I would propose that two systems of awards be developed—the first dealing entirely with degrees as statements of intellectual interest and experience, and the second dealing with credentials that are based on proficiency and are job related and job predictive. If this were to be implemented, it would mean that there would be nothing particularly unreasonable in a policeman getting a degree in philosophy. His credentialing as a policeman would be handled through an entirely separate system and would not have to be based on his having acquired a college degree. On the other hand, his intellectual interest in philosophy would not be hampered by the vocationally oriented credentialing system. This system would help to solve the problem of the strong and unwelcome relationship between general and liberal educational levels and occupational status placement levels. There is no particular reason why a person who seeks a blue-collar job should be limited in his intellectual interests. The lack of access to intellectual interests forced on certain occupational groups is one of the chief ways whereby our social-class system perpetuates itself.

Indeed, one of the major sources of malaise in contemporary American life may be the rapidly increasing boredom and lack of self-fulfillment permeating the world of work.[1] During the 1950s, ours was an almost pathologically work-oriented society, and one's work virtually determined social status. Today, however, much evidence has accumulated that people need a diversity of status characteristics which could be provided through a separation of intellectual interests from the credentialing process itself.

Many trends in higher education today support this move. The large number of nondegree students, the Regents' Degree in New York, the Capital University Center in Connecticut, the ability of the Arthur D. Little Co. to grant the master's degree in business administration, and many of the "new colleges" described in Larry Hall's excellent new book entitled *The New Colleges* (Jossey-Bass, 1973)—these are all steps toward freeing the credentialing process. The access must be broadened both ways. There must be broader access to higher education for those who simply wish to investigate or study some area of human life that intrigues them without any concern for their occupational mobility, and better access to the credentialing process for those who do not have a great deal of exposure to higher education but possess skills they wish to have applied to occupational advancement.

I do not wish to suggest that we eliminate credentialism. Every society—from the primitive hunting cultures to advanced western technological nations—has to have some filtration system for making sure that individuals qualify for important roles and functions. No one wants to fly with an unlicensed pilot, even one who holds several Ph.D. degrees and scored in the 780s on the Graduate Record Examination. There is, of course, a vast and interesting symbol system that goes

[1] *Work in America,* Report of a Special Task Force to the Secretary of Health, Education, and Welfare (Cambridge, Mass.: MIT Press, 1973). Also see James O'Toole's contribution to this book.

along with the credentialing process in most cultures. But the system in the United States has become vague, and the B.A. degree is at best a proxy credential and does not indicate anything specific about an individual's competence level.[2] One potential exception should be noted, and that is the competency-based curricula, both for college-wide objectives and for the completion of the major.

If occupational credentialing is removed from higher education, who will handle it and how? I would propose that the federal government provide initial funding for five regional examining institutes. These institutes will not offer courses but rather develop and administer examinations to qualify individuals in a variety of competency levels, both for degrees (which may or may not be job related) and for specific certification of job-related skills. Tests developed by the regional examining institutes should be criterion-referenced tests unless there is a specific reason for wanting nationally normed test results. Use should be made of alternative-evaluation strategies such as games and simulations, in-basket tests, and many demonstration techniques, as well as written multiple-choice strategies. Criterion-referenced testing provides much more diagnostic information for both the person taking the test and any agency that might be interested in hiring him. When norm-referencing must be done, the norms could be standardized on other individuals who are proficient in performing that specific function satisfactorily.

In addition to the development of criterion-referenced testing procedures, the regional examining institutes could play an important diagnostic and counseling function. Corporations with jobs to offer might want counseling on the proper criteria for making a selection of applicants. The general public might want to use institute services to find a new job, to determine progress toward personal educational objectives, or to plan improvement.

In addition, the regional examining institute should be able to handle questions of academic equivalency testing. In most of these areas, strong support and collaboration will have to exist between the regional examining institute, educational associations, and public and private institutions of higher education. It is automatically assumed that the REIs will become a bridge between higher education and the occupational and vocational world. Such an agency should dedicate

[2] David McClelland, "Testing for Competence Rather Than 'Intelligence,'" *American Psychologist,* January, 1973.

itself to performing those evaluative functions and certifying operations which are not currently being supplied by existing agencies. For example, the regional examining institute might well function as an evaluation development unit for an existing agency that wants to develop a new test. Product development, then, would be an important function of the regional examining institute.

In the development of evaluation procedures, not only should the academic world be represented but also individuals who could be described as *distinguished practitioners*. In dentistry, those professors who no longer deal with actual patients are known by practitioners as *dry-finger* dentists. For examinations dealing with proficiency in dentistry, one would assume that both the practitioner and the professor should be included as important agents in developing tests. Similarly, the community organizer and the professor of social work should meet on equal terms.

The initiation of such a regional examining institute probably can not be left to any single state. However, agencies such as the Education Commission of the States, the Western Interstate Commission on Higher Education, the Southern Regional Education Board, and the New England Board for Higher Education could serve as the initial coordinating units. Once the regional examining institutes have been established, it might well be that small user fees could allow the federal-support base to decline systematically. Certainly if one looks at the fees charged to students for taking the Graduate Record Examination, it is clear that user fees could be a similar possibility for revenue.

The regional examining institute would also be a good place to house a student credit bank. One function of such a credit bank would be an equivalency transcript service, in which students who have off-campus creditable experience or who have done work at several colleges can receive credit that would be contained in a central record file. This file could be used both for degrees and credentials. To avoid problems about the confidentiality of these records, the student should have complete control over the process, which is not the case in some colleges and universities. The REI may also play an advocacy role for its clients in some situations.

Some critics might contend that the regional examining institute will increase the reliance on credentialing in our society. On the contrary, the regional examining institute could make credentialing a more honest and effective process by making sure that the credentials actually mean something and by separating degrees and credentials. In addition, the diversity of functions proposed for the regional examining institute should indicate to most people that the primary function of the REI will be to serve the needs of individuals—those applying for jobs, those with jobs to offer, those who wish a record of their academic progress in the form of a degree, and those who simply want more feedback on their own particular performance for their own particular reasons. Within such a context, we might well begin the evolution of a truly sophisticated and open-access counseling system, an area which is badly needed in American higher education and American life generally.

Another argument certain to be raised has to do with the possibility of the regional examining institute homogenizing instruction as people attempt to teach for the tests. One reply is that if the tests are handled in a creative way, with the use of increasing alternatives to multiple-choice, standardized examinations, this process can be at least partially eliminated. For example, in driver-education courses, everyone knows that the student will spend some time in a driving simulator, but nobody tries to cheat by teaching the simulator. To do so would be a theoretical impossibility, as with in-basket and other simulations. On the other hand, if the final examination in driver education is simply a multiple-choice test, it is quite easy to teach for that. As the evaluation devices get more specific and more diverse, the possibility of teaching for the test becomes less likely.

A great many of the new dimensions of education in America suggest that the time has come for the regional examining institute; such new dimensions include newspaper and television courses, academic experiences that are not courselike in their nature, and other academic experiences that are not offered for credit.

16

Networks and Quality

Morris T. Keeton

T alk about learning networks often focuses on lowering costs and increasing resources. The potential of networks for increasing learning opportunities and enhancing the quality of learning is often either overlooked or assumed.

The library resources and services of America are moving at a brisk pace toward becoming a public-utility network with open access to all. The Periodical Bank of the Associated Colleges of the Midwest is a straw in the wind; it now serves forty-four user institutions (initially it had ten members) with fifty thousand periodical titles compared to the two thousand made accessible by the initial members.[1] What is that resource doing for the quality of learning opportunities

[1] *Acquainter,* American Association for Higher Education, February, 1974.

in the forty-four user institutions? No doubt each institution can spend less on periodicals and claim access to vastly more periodicals than would otherwise have been provided. But are faculty and students seeing and using the resources to enhance learning?

It is time for accrediting and evaluating bodies to stop asking how many periodicals, books, and nonprint media an institution owns and begin asking what quality and quantity of resources the institution actually provides. How fast and adequate is the access? How imaginatively, thoroughly, and effectively are the resources being used?

Let us imagine that ours is going to become, and ought to become, a learning society in the sense that practically all citizens will need to continue learning throughout their lives. Let us imagine that much of this learning will be playful, since many will have come to enjoy learning and to be curious about many things. Much of the learning, we will imagine, will also be useful for understanding and acting on issues of public policy and personal choice. Still other learning will be directly useful in people's work and in sustaining or enhancing their competence for economically productive or rewarding work throughout life.

Let us hope, but not be too sanguine in expecting, that a growing proportion of this learning will be self-directed. The learner's own vocational interests, his citizen concerns, his personal hobbies, and his priorities in other respects will activate his inquiries and direct his calls upon the retrieval capabilities of our systems for meeting his learning needs. An enormous problem will then arise, and the full capacity of all the possible networks will be required to cope with this problem: How can we best help this learner—and a multitude of others—find, understand, interpret, and apply what they need from the overabundance of stored intellectual treasure? In other words, how can we provide the human resources needed to guide learners in their use of existing intellectual resources?

A function of networks is to enlarge the pool of resources to meet the demand. In the case of periodical journals, easy and inexpensive duplication provides the satisfaction of demand for an unlimited number of users. The problem merely requires that we preserve and enlarge the basic treasure and keep the duplication and distribution machinery increasing to meet the demand.

With human resources, the capacity of networks to satisfy growing demand is more difficult and more expensive. Since we seem to be approaching the limits of what tuition-payers and taxpayers can afford for learning, we will have to develop ways that avoid substantial rises in cost.

The most economical networks are not those of like institutions, but networks of unlike ones with complementary needs. Such networks permit a mutually beneficial exchange of resources and services with little or no increase in aggregate costs. For example, a university seeking an effective learning option in regional economic and environmental planning could link up with a regional planning commission seeking a pool of talent for its task. By combining budgets for their respective purposes, these dissimilar institutions can both do a better job. To coordinate this interplay and to exploit it for each purpose will either add costs or require reallocations within the two programs to meet the new costs. A similar symbiosis can be achieved in a law school using a law firm or a network of legal-service instrumentalities; a medical service collaborating with a medical school; a community-development program joining forces with a social-science research and instructional program and a media studies program; or a group of small industries joining forces with an undergraduate school of administration and a computer-services facility.

The effectiveness of such networks results from efficient institutions joining each other to gain new qualitative achievements at still higher levels of efficiency. This permits greater educational resources per student without driving up the cost. Such strategies work best where the learning is achieved in part by having the student do socially productive work in the domain of the cooperating institution; if the employer demands costworthy service from the student and pays him a salary, a further social benefit exists in the increment to gross national product and in the student earning an income while he learns. Such cooperation is still relatively rare because of the problems and costs of coordination and because of the political problems of obtaining sanction and equitable cost-sharing. We may find a greater readiness to confront the political and managerial costs of bringing these networks into being as economic pressure increases toward efficiency and as political pressure increases toward a better life.

Other kinds of networks ought to grow and are likely to grow in the future; for example, combinations of like institutions that alone do not have some of the efficiencies possible in combination. Many of these combinations form around a single purpose such as improvement in the efficiency or the effectiveness of development services, admissions and financial-aid services, curriculum development, faculty development, international studies, instruction in chosen areas, and fund raising. Rapid development is certain for the legislatively mandated systems of statewide coordination and control of both public and private postsecondary education—this despite a major struggle around the apparently conflicting values of institutional autonomy and statewide coordination.

Ideally, any university should be a network taking advantage of various strategies for economy, efficiency, and quality. In fact, most such systems have fallen prey to tendencies toward overextensions (taking on functions that are not efficient for the unit), poor coordination (failing to make the potentially collaborating parts collaborate), overloading of central costs, and exploitation of some parts by other parts due to political or other factors. The same hazards lie in wait for new consortia and networks, however idealistically conceived.

The rising need for quality and efficiency, and the growing body of experience with the problems as well as the potentials of networks, should result in greater effort to monitor and evaluate network performance. If the growing state and federal controls on postsecondary education are to be prevented from stifling competition and enterprise in the field, there will probably have to be other means of accountability that give more promise than centralized controls and the preauditing of every fiscal and programatic venture.

So far we have dealt only with instrumentation, but what about purposes and priorities? I am very skeptical of educational plans that continue to segregate career preparation from liberal education. That segregation works to the detriment of both purposes, for theory uninformed by direct experience is poor theory, and work unguided by the values and concepts of liberal education is likely to be ill-chosen and ill-executed. There is hardly an intellectual task more difficult than that of integrating ideas, values, and data drawn from diverse sources into a coherent perspective. I propose that our society needs an increasing number and potency of networks of unlike members, bringing together people of diverse and even competing interests and outlooks, not only to join resources in facilitating learning but also to think through together what is most worth learning and doing.

The early efforts of man to fly were frustrated in part by his failure to imagine what enormous power would be required to lift aircraft for effective flight. To realize the human potential of a learning society, a similar flight of imagination about resources will be required. To muster those resources and bring them effectively to the service of learners will in turn require a most ingenious use of networks, with like and unlike institutions serving to store and make accessible the intellectual heritage. Once we learn to make educational networks fly, new options of purpose and possibility will also emerge—and we will be obliged to replace our old visions with new ones.

17

Toward a National Counseling System

Robin Scott Wilson

$\mathbf{M}$ost of us are already familiar with the severity and ubiquity of the student mobility problem. About one out of four American college students makes at least one change in school location; he seldom does so with ease. In addition, growing numbers of more mature Americans seek re-entry into the postsecondary system after some years out of it. Still others—their desire for education and certification sharpened by learning in proprietary schools and military- or industrial-training programs—stand at the admission officer's door rapping to get in, asking for some institutional recognition of the fact that hard knocks still have some educational value.

The transfer problem is part of the broader problem of admissions; of matching individual skills, aspirations, accomplishments, potentials, and buying power to institutional entrance and certification requirements, most of which have been designed primarily for continuing students. This stable group is more amenable to broad statistical definition and less finely discriminating selection criteria.

But in fact no two students are alike, just as no two institutions are alike. The problem of matching students with institutions—for either entry or subsequent re-entry as transfer or adult students—defies rational analysis in terms other than Werner Heisenberg's uncertainty principle, which is splendid for electrons but something less than humane for people.

The postsecondary educational establishment is trying to meet the transfer problem, although its best efforts are likely to be piecemeal. Some institutions, under the economic pressure of declining enrollments, are likely to be a bit more flexible in evaluating learning experiences from unorthodox or unfamiliar sources. State coordinating boards, their proliferation a burgeoning phenomenon which is yet to reach full flower, are working hard to join disparate public institutions into articulated systems. National associations will publish analyses and exhortations; accrediting commissions will circulate entreaties; and the federal government will move closer to the principle that the aid dollar follows the student wherever he goes. These efforts will produce change, doubtless slowly and with great uncertainty. Meanwhile individual faculty in charge of departmental and college standards of admission move in orbits largely uncoordinated with national or regional efforts—to the detriment of individual students.

Is there a national solution to the problems arising from the new student mobility? Certainly one solution would be to eliminate differences among institutions and structure postsecondary education into one glistening monolithic apparatus, capable of turning out well-trained (if not well-educated) young men and women with great efficiency—and to hell with anyone who is not proper grist for the mill. The threatened demise of the private college under current economic onslaughts, coupled with a move toward mandatory federal accreditation, could in time make such a nightmare approach reality.

Such a solution, brought about by massive pressures from above, is clearly unacceptable. But how about a solution that comes about, not from national fiat, but from the consumer pressure of six or seven million people with educational aspirations? Is it possible to inject a new force to alleviate the hardships of student mobility and the pressure of the marketplace?

We have a global working model. The world is united by an amazingly intricate combination of public and private agencies; it is their business to move people safely and rapidly from one place to another and see that they are housed, fed, insured, and entertained, all at a broad range of costs. Almost all of these agencies are publicly chartered and regulated in some fashion, almost all are competitive, all publish their offerings and readily modify them—within broad limits imposed by considerations of health and safety—in response to consumer demand. Equipped with a sophisticated and truly global information system, a good travel agent can determine a traveler's needs and desires, his budget and time limitations. From this information the agent can arrange a complex tour that may involve a half-dozen common carriers, tickets to Disney World, lodging in Mrs. Glutz' Bide-A-Wee Tourist Home, and dinner for four twenty-seven kilometers south of Dijon. The agent can make arrangements to fly one to Madrid, transfer to a train for Andorra, and there book a burro for a pack trip into the Pyrenees. And should our traveler, saddlesore from the trip, ask his local travel agent to cancel his reservation at the Bodensee and get him on a flight to the sedentary delights of London, the chances are good that the agent could do it.

If travel can be coordinated this way, why can't American postsecondary education? We have licensed, or otherwise chartered and regulated, all sorts of brokers in our society: those who explicate the mysterious ways of God to man, those who mediate between us and the law, and those who negotiate our relations with our own livers. How many full-time trained and licensed counselors—independent of institutional fealties, concerned only with the consumer's best interests —mediate between us and our polymorphic system of postsecondary education?

Not very many.

Let us examine, then, the feasibility of establishing a national system of educational brokers who have been trained to serve potential students of postsecondary education and who have at their fingertips current and accurate information on all the postsecondary educational opportunities for which a given client might qualify. Such a system would place a skilled counselor and his information devices in every village, town, and metropolitan subdivision—perhaps in the local public library. These counselors could also make use of such existing channels as county extension offices, vocational-rehabilitation services, and public welfare and employment agencies.

These Public Postsecondary Educational Counselors would be united by an elaborate data-processing and information-retrieval system, one aspect of which would be similar to that used by airlines to confirm instantly the availability of space. Counselors would be prepared to administer diagnostic and competency tests to help clients more clearly define their educational needs and vocational aspirations. These trained people would be able to insert into the information system all the particulars of the client's wishes—financial, geographical, vocational, and intellectual—and come up with a relatively brief list of appropriate institutions and availability details. Our counselors would be responsible only to their clients and their own bureaucracy. Lamentably, this plan would involve the creation of a new bureaucracy of substantial proportions.

It might reasonably be argued that such a pervasive and obviously expensive system would raise more problems than it would solve. Unquestionably, getting such a massive effort organized, staffed, and funded would involve, if not a sea of troubles, a good-sized lake of them. Still, the necessary manpower would seem to be at hand in the large numbers of educators for whom teaching jobs are unavailable. There are many men and women with first-hand experience in postsecondary education who, with a modicum of special training, might find their roles as independent educational brokers challenging and fulfilling.

Such people would not come cheap; counseling is not a profession for second-raters. But salary costs might well be borne in part by the patrons, who could expect to be spared the direct costs of multiple applications and the far greater indirect costs of entering the wrong institution or chasing vain vocational aspirations. Postsecondary institutions might also bear part of the cost since their own counseling loads would be lessened and since the institutions would be spared some of the hidden costs of misplaced and frustrated students.

The associated information system would also come dear— data banks, dedicated lines, and terminal equipment are not yet available in discount houses. But much of the information service could be put to additional uses—the acquisition and storage of comparable administrative data for institutional planners, availability of up-to-date admissions information, avoidance of duplication and uncertainty as institutions recruit with increasing competitiveness from a single and perhaps diminishing pool of potential students. Of course, one should approach a proposal for such a system with a certain wariness, a wise suspicion of the simplistic, the pervasive, and the bureaucratic. No one wants to run the risk of building another organizational Frankenstein's monster, a kind of educational IRS.

Perhaps there is reassurance in considering the governance of the system. However funded, should it be organized and administered on a state-by-state basis? Perhaps, but educational opportunities and the movements of students are increasingly free of state citizenship restrictions. Should it, then, be administered on a national basis by the federal government, like Social Security and Medicare? Perhaps, but our recent national experience with centrally administered experiments in social engineering have not been uniformly happy.

The answer may be that the proposed national counseling system might best be organized along regional lines—with strong interconnections—and administered by public boards made up of representatives from professional organizations, governments, consortia or other aggregations of postsecondary institutions, accrediting commissions, educational associations, student and faculty groups, and a few taxpaying citizens scattered about to keep the rest honest. Such broad representation might be unwieldy, but it would help preserve the essential independence of the counselor, while providing broad policy guidance, as he seeks to make the best possible match between student and institution.

It would be interesting if someone could be persuaded to apply techniques of computer-modeling to such a proposed national counseling system. Perhaps we would find that the system would be far too cumbersome and expensive—a kind of organizational dinosaur, vast of appetite, tiny of brain. Or we might find that savings would come close to offsetting costs and that the public would enthusiastically welcome a friend in the higher educational court. In either case, it would be good to know. If we are indeed moving from a society dedicated to the production of more and more goods and services to a society dedicated to the notion of life-long learning, of individual personal, intellectual, and aesthetic development—then perhaps even an expensive system might be justified in terms of a greater social good.

18

Community-Based Guidance

Nancy K. Schlossberg

Many adults, and young people as well, are unsure of what they really want out of life and of where and how to get it. Though some developmental theorists have postulated that life consists of a series of distinct and sequential stages, it is more realistic to view life—and especially adulthood—as a number of role transformations in four basic areas: vocation, parenthood, intimacy, and community. Some changes are fraught with anticipation, hope, and eagerness; others, with apprehension, fear, and depression. One theme, however, seems common to all role transformations: that of stock-taking.

This reassessment often leads to anxiety and despair, particularly among people between thirty and sixty, since it often seems to be their last chance. Moreover, some may feel that they have not measured up to the ideals they set for themselves earlier and have lost the opportunity of doing so. The situation is aggravated because it is commonly assumed that the middle-aged know themselves, have resolved their problems, and are relatively stable and rational human beings. This assumption, coupled with the inattention that our society gives to middle age, contributes to tremendous feelings of inadequacy on the part of many adults. They may feel that they are unique in the negative sense, immature, or neurotic.

More and more adult men and women of all ages, races, and walks of life are confronted by a confusing welter of *what ifs* and *if onlys:* "What if I had known earlier that women could be women as well as engineers?" "If only I had not entered the family insurance business." "If only I had completed high school." Usually, these are the cries of people who have already made basic decisions about education, career, and life style and who feel that there is no turning back. There are other questions that plague adults as well—questions that may indicate little psychic pain and turmoil but are equally urgent if the individual is not to be crippled in achieving full development: "Where is a school with part-time training in tailoring?" "Is there an opportunity for women morticians?" "What are the options for someone with my interests?" These people suffer not from the crisis brought about by role transformation but from an information void.

Whatever the questions asked—whether they relate to one's identity or to the availability of educational and occupational opportunities—many adults will not be able to find the answers on their own. They cannot turn to the educational system, for they are outside of it. It seems clear that at any given time more of the population is out of the educational system than is in it. According to 1970 census figures, about 46 percent of the total U.S. population is between twenty-five and sixty-five years old; this age group comprises a large number of people who may need and want educational and career counseling but who have no easy way of getting it. Even the ever-increasing number of adults for whom education is a continuing or recurring event spend a great deal of time outside the system. Many adults, then, must make important educational and career decisions in a vacuum, without the kind of help that they may desperately require.

The groups outside the system to which guidance and counseling services might be particularly helpful are varied. Some of the more obvious ones are dropouts, transfer students, veterans, women re-entering the labor market, men and women at mid-career shifts, and retired persons (some of the latter still relatively young). Let us take a look at some of the data on these groups.

Young people may drop out of the educational system—temporarily or permanently—at various points: before high-school graduation, between high-school graduation and college, during the college years. John C. Flanagan, reporting data from his Project TALENT, notes that although almost half of all eleventh graders in 1960 and 1970 planned to attend college, only half of this group will actually receive a college degree. Thus thousands of students are "forced to modify their plans" and drop out of the system.[1] In addition to the dropouts, one in four college students transfers from one institution to another at some point.[2] In most cases, the institutions from which these students depart probably give them no help in selecting another institution. As for veterans, between 1964 and 1971, five million men (and a much smaller number of women) were discharged from the armed services, and one out of every ten had not received even a high-school diploma.[3] Many of these veterans may want further schooling but have nowhere to turn for guidance.

Information is harder to come by on other groups—women who want to re-enter the labor force when they are freed from child-rearing responsibilities, adults of both sexes who want to change their occupations, retired persons—but some idea of their numbers can be gained by the indirect evidence of adult education enrollment figures. According to an article in *Guidepost*, "One of every fifty men and women thirty-five or older is going back to school," most of them on a part-time basis.[4] Over half of these are women, although at the undergraduate level men outnumber women. If these adults represent the proportion of persons who have been successful in continuing their education, how many more adults may there be in the population who would probably return if they had adequate guidance?

It would seem reasonable to conclude, then, that large numbers of people in the country want to go back to school or change jobs or both. It would also seem reasonable to conclude that large numbers

[1] John C. Flanagan, "Some Pertinent Findings of Project TALENT." *Vocational Guidance Quarterly,* December, 1973.

[2] Reported in the Airlie House Conference on College Transfer, December 4, 1973.

[3] Stephen K. Bailey, Francis U. Macy, and Donn Vickers, *Alternative Paths to the High School Diploma,* Reston, Virginia: National Association of Secondary School Principals, 1973, p. 37.

[4] American Personnel and Guidance Association, February 11, 1974.

of people in school are in the process of reformulating plans and clarifying goals. Clearly, a genuine need exists to link systematically the people (the largest proportion of whom are out of the system) with the available resources.

The frequent failure of the professional to discharge this basic function usually stems neither from the mediocrity of the professional nor from the inadequacy of counselor education, though in particular cases both defects doubtless mar performance. Rather, it stems first from the systemic deficiency already discussed: Too many people are outside the educational system, and they are unable to find someone trained to help them answer such questions as "Where am I going?" and "How do I get there?" Second, it stems from structural weaknesses within the educational system that lead to inadequate delivery of guidance even to those who can make use of that system. Although guidance is intended to serve and to liberate individuals, too often the practice has been to serve and maintain the system.

Many studies of the counselor role in public schools corroborate this point. More time is spent in administering and scheduling, in what may be called "lunchroom, toiletroom duty," than is spent in interacting with students about their goals and the ways to reach them. Summarizing the results of the few major evaluations of guidance, Eli Ginzberg wrote: "School counselors appear to spend the bulk of their time in approving courses of study, in assisting with college applications, in dealing with rule infractions, and in test adminstration. Few spend a significant amount of time in activities specifically designed to lead to improved decision-making and long-range planning, the express goals of guidance."[5] In fact, according to one study cited by Ginzberg, "over two-thirds of the girls and more than three-quarters of the boys who were planning to work after high school reported that they had never discussed their occupational plans with a guidance counselor."

To students, the counselor's role is perceived as maintenance of the system; to counselor educators, the counselor's role is perceived as facilitating students' effective career decisions; to legislators, the counselor's role is perceived as ranging from identifying the talented to stimulating the disadvantaged, depending on apparent national needs; and to counselors themselves, the role wavers from satisfying the school administration to passing courses at universities to helping the overwhelming number of students who pass through the office. The dys-

[5] Eli Ginzberg, *Career Guidance: Who Needs It, Who Provides It, Who Can Improve It* (New York: McGraw-Hill Book Company, 1971), pp. 267–268.

function of counseling in many educational settings and the unavailability of counseling outside the educational system argues for a thorough reconsideration of this process.

The problems of isolation from the educational system and its services and the dysfunctions within the present system might be solved if guidance centers were independent of any control by educational institutions although free to draw upon their resources. The guidance centers would be open to any and all clients in the community. Those people who are now outside the educational system would have somewhere to turn for help in identifying and clarifying their educational and occupational goals and in finding ways to reach those goals.

The community-based guidance counselors would act as educational brokers between clients and resources, their primary duty being to serve the client rather than maintain the system. As independent professionals, the counselors would be in a position to push particular institutions in ways, and with a wholeheartedness, that would be impossible if the institutions were their employers. For example, the community-based counselor could bring to bear moral or legal pressure that might force institutions to rethink old notions and modify antiquated or irrelevant rules. A shift in locale—from school base to community—would move counselor loyalty from the institution to the individual.

Several years ago, I was one of several members of the College Entrance Examination Board Commission on Tests who urged that the Board establish regional guidance centers to act as "advocative, protective, and supportive" agencies outside the established structures. Such agencies were to be based on the legal conception of the ombudsman—one who helps and even protects an individual citizen in encounters with agents of government. At that time, the proposal was branded as "totally unrealistic." What then was seen as a pie-in-the-sky project has since become a reality in several places.

One example of a plan in action for brokering people and resources is the Regional Learning Service (RLS) of Central New York, an agency that serves five counties. Reaching out to persons of all ages and educational backgrounds who want to earn a high-school diploma or college degree, to change careers, to clarify goals, or simply to gain more knowledge, the RLS uses learning consultants to help clients select their goals and plan an appropriate educational program. In addition, the consultant follows up on the clients to give them additional aid, for instance, by putting them in touch with other people whose interests are similar to their own. Because RLS works in cooperation with (though independent of) other educational programs in New York state, the Regents External Degrees program, for instance, it can be particularly useful in having the individual's previous experience evaluated and accredited. The learning consultants are selected not on the basis of their academic background and credentials but on the basis of their personal qualities, and they are put through a training program that in large part focuses on developing their informational skills. Altogether, the RLS would seem to be a successful nontraditional approach to guidance.

A slightly different approach is illustrated in the Community College of Vermont, an institution with neither a campus nor a full-time faculty. Established to serve a dispersed rural population, the college tailors both course offerings and scheduling to the demands of the students. According to the *Carnegie Quarterly,* Fall 1973, "Counseling is the key to making this type of system work," and counselors actively keep in touch with students by telephone, maintain an open-door policy, and arrange for group get-togethers. The counselors also offer teaching-method guidance to the teachers, many of whom are employed at more traditional kinds of colleges or in occupations outside the academic world.

Still in its formative stages, the Career Counseling and Guidance Project of the National Institute of Education is aimed at home-based adults in the Providence, Rhode Island, area. The primary purpose of the project is to provide information, principally by telephone, about education, training, and careers to persons who may want to re-enter the labor force. Heavy emphasis is being placed on evaluating this program to see whether it serves a real existing need, whether such unusual methods as telephone guidance services and mobile career information centers are workable, whether the program succeeds in encouraging clients to enroll in educational or training programs which lead to employment, and whether it succeeds in developing the client's ability to perform a job search.

All three of these projects—though differing considerably in their scope, methods, and stage of development—represent at least an approximation of the ideal of community-based guidance. Scattered throughout the country are other innovative programs. Most of them are funded through private sources, though some of them receive federal subsidies. Women's centers are springing up on college campuses everywhere; most of these programs exist outside the regular institutional guidance system and are aimed at facilitating women's re-entry into the world of work. A movement toward providing nontraditional kinds of guidance seems well underway.

The idea of community-based guidance is catching on. Actual programs are in operation. What we need now is imagination, coupled with a grasp of the political realities, to devise workable strategies for implementing such programs on a national scale.

PART FOUR

Issues in Academe

The problems taken up in Part Four are more clearly internal in nature. Three of them—affirmative action, tenure, and unionization—are discussed in a single chapter by Richard Chait and Andrew T. Ford, who point out how solutions that might work for one of these problems can easily aggravate one or both of the others. Comparing the relationship of the three to a "lovers' triangle," with higher education in the middle, the authors believe that "the likelihood that all three forces will survive intact is slight indeed." Their conclusions about which of the forces will prevail at certain points in the conflict are tied closely to the legal consequences of various courses of action.

Unionization, or collective bargaining, is also the subject of two other chapters in this section. Linda Bond considers its impact on students, and Neil S. Bucklew examines how bargaining affects aca-

demic policymaking. For both authors, negotiation about "conditions of employment" is seen as having potentially great bearing on conditions of learning and thus reaching well beyond what might be considered the exclusive domain of faculty. Bond believes that students must somehow get into the bargaining act—directly or indirectly—or the agreements will be unacceptable to them. For Bucklew, the answer lies more in limiting the scope of matters included in a bargaining contract so that the deliberative, consultative nature of academic policymaking is not sacrificed.

The two chapters that follow deal with the increasingly tenuous —or "nontenurous"—relationship between faculty and their jobs. Myron J. Lunine reports on an alternative to tenure that is being tried at Hampshire College, and James L. Bess outlines a scheme for redirecting surplus or dissatisfied faculty into new careers that would benefit not only them but their institutions and society. Both authors seem to reject the prevailing "zero-sum" philosophy which holds that one party has to lose for another to gain. As they see it, all have something to gain once a spirit of cooperation and trust is established.

Financing is not so much an internal problem as a condition of existence which effects all internal problems. Higher education has lived with the legislation enacted in 1972 long enough to begin thinking about and moving toward a position on legislation for 1976. It is from this juncture—about midway between the old laws and the new —that Ben Lawrence offers his proposals on the general shape and direction of future policy on financial support. His recommendations, and the reasoning behind them, differ significantly from some of the more widely discussed positions being advanced and should serve to enliven the debate as the new legislation begins to be hammered out.

In the concluding chapter of this volume, Harold L. Enarson, a university president who knows first hand the thousand natural shocks administrators are heir to, catalogs all the forces that seem to be eroding the capacity of presidents to lead, or even sustain, their institutions. He asks, "What is left to govern?" It would not be fair to give away his response to that question, but if you've been down in the mouth lately about the prospects of higher education, by all means read it.

WILLIAM FERRIS

19

Affirmative Action, Tenure, and Unionization

Richard Chait, Andrew T. Ford

L̶ike a lovers' triangle, the three-sided relationship that includes affirmative action, tenure, and unionization foreshadows contention. All interests cannot be mutually accommodated. Where overlap occurs, conflict will arise. And as with the lovers' triangle, the likelihood is slight indeed that all three forces will survive intact.

Federally mandated affirmative-action programs have altered traditional college and university personnel practices substantially.

Portions of this chapter appeared in *The Chronicle of Higher Education*, October 1, 1973, p. 16.

Affirmative action has prompted college administrators to revamp recruitment procedures and revise other personnel practices such as promotions, retentions, transfers, and salary scales. While affirmative action has had a critical impact upon these areas, the most significant ramification may be yet to come. Compliance with affirmative-action regulations may well end, or at least drastically transform, the most established and distinctive personnel practice of academe—tenure.

Once awarded academic tenure by a particular college or university, a faculty member holds a continuous appointment at that institution until retirement or voluntary resignation. Tenure may be revoked only for "adequate cause," financial exigencies, or to meet significant program changes. To receive tenure, a faculty member must satisfy minimum eligibility requirements, demonstrate a certain performance level, and reveal adequate potential for growth and development. As traditionally used, all three bases for awarding tenure apparently conflict with affirmative-action guidelines.

Institutions of higher education usually cast minimum eligibility requirements for tenure in terms of experience, academic credentials, and rank. Although specific criteria to determine eligibility for tenure vary widely, several are commonly applied. For example, faculty must generally serve a three- to seven-year probationary period that usually follows graduate school. Herein lies the first apparent conflict with affirmative action.

The typical assistant professor, perhaps twenty-six to thirty-two years old, has between three and seven years to demonstrate worthiness for tenure. Yet these years coincide very nearly with the years women usually bear children and remain at home with the preschoolers. Female faculty, then, are considerably disadvantaged by the probationary requirement as maternal responsibilities may temporarily interrupt service, slow professional growth, and limit scholarly productivity. Consequently, women faculty members may present less persuasive records than male counterparts. While stopgap measures such as maternity leaves and extended probationary periods have become more commonplace, women still remain handicapped by present procedures. Florence Moog, professor of biology at Washington University, correctly concludes that beyond the doctorate the tenure system constitutes the foremost barrier for the female scholar. Should the courts agree that these procedures unlawfully discriminate against women or violate affirmative-action guidelines, the probationary period as currently applied will will have to be modified or perhaps abolished, as Ms. Moog suggests.[1]

Credentials as a criterion for tenure also seem to be at odds with affirmative action, since federal regulations prohibit the application of evaluative criteria that either tend to perpetuate a previously discriminatory situation or that do not relate to job performance. In a 1971 decision, Griggs v. Duke Power Company, the Supreme Court invalidated a company policy that required a high-school diploma and a passing score on a general intelligence test for employment and promotion. Insofar as neither condition could be manifestly related to job performance, the court ruled that the stipulations violated the 1964 Civil Rights Act.

Whether these practices were deliberately or inadvertently discriminatory had no relevance, since the act specified that good intent "does not redeem employment practices or testing mechanisms that operate as 'built-in headwinds' for minority groups and are unrelated to measuring job capability." Indeed, the court struck at the very heart of credentialism. "The facts of this case," the court asserted, "demonstrate the inadequacy of broad and general testing devices as well as the infirmity of using diplomas or degrees as fixed measures of capability."[2]

If the Griggs case appears too far removed from the educational realm, consider a recent lower federal court decision, Armstead v. Starkville Municipal School District.[3] In this instance, the court declared a public-school board had unlawfully discriminated against blacks by tying teachers' appointments and retention to the attainment of a master's degree and specified scores on Graduate Record Examinations that had not been validated as accurate predictors of job performance.

These cases plainly establish legal precedents and principles readily transferable to college faculties and to criteria used for awarding tenure, which is, after all, a condition of employment. Colleges

[1] Florence Moog, "Women, Students, and Tenure," *Science,* 174, December 3, 1971, 983.

[2] *Griggs v. Duke Power Company,* 401 U.S. 424; 91 S. Ct. 849 (1971).

[3] *Armstead v. Starkville Municipal School District,* 325 F. Supp. 560 (1971).

and universities that hope to maintain present practice must be prepared to demonstrate that conventional criteria—a terminal degree or its equivalent, a given probationary period, and a particular rank—are manifestly related to job performance. Colleges must substantiate these contentions because the Griggs decision held that "Congress has placed on the employer the burden of showing that any given requirement must have a manifest relationship to the employment in question."

The implications of Griggs and related decisions are not limited to minimum eligibility requirements for tenure; traditional methods of judging performance and potential are also affected. Colleges and universities must be able to show that they use meaningful, concrete, nondiscriminatory procedures and instruments for evaluating teaching performance. If only lip service is paid to teaching and what really counts is the candidate's publication record, then the institution, as the employer, must be able to prove that the publications are "demonstrably" related to the job, which is teaching. Similar arguments will have to be advanced if potential is evaluated on the basis of present performance or on meeting minimum eligibility requirements.

But affirmative action will affect far more than the criteria employed to award tenure. In 1972, colleges and universities with tenure systems (85 percent of the total) had a median of 41 percent to 50 percent of their faculties on tenure. In the spring of 1971, 41 percent of the respondents to a Keast Commission survey awarded tenure to all eligible faculty members, and two-thirds awarded tenure to 70 percent or more of those under consideration.[4] At this rate many schools will soon have faculties solidified by a very high proportion of tenured personnel. A faculty solidified by tenure stands at cross-purposes with affirmative action, which requires more fluidity to be effective. To appoint more blacks, chicanos, women, and other persons previously victimized by discrimination requires vacancies. In the current no-growth era, vacancies must arise largely from turnover rather than expansion. Tenure, however, limits turnover.

Unionization also threatens the traditional practice of tenure. Although rejected by some faculties, unionization currently enjoys substantial support, especially among "lower-tier" institutions and

[4] Commission on Academic Tenure in Higher Education, *Faculty Tenure: A Report and Recommendations by the Commission on Academic Tenure in Higher Education* (San Francisco: Jossey-bass, 1973), p. 4.

junior faculty.[5] By the fall of 1973, 212 postsecondary institutions had collective bargaining agents.[6]

Whereas affirmative action challenges the criteria and procedures used to award tenure, unions challenge tenure by addressing its traditional purposes: employment security and the protection of academic freedom. As an alternative route to job security, unionization is likely to supplant tenure if only because it is more effective. Unions aim to protect everyone within the bargaining unit; tenure protects only the tenured. Unions seek to provide immediate job security; tenure requires a probationary period and affords little protection to probationary personnel. Unions shift the burden of proof onto management—employees are presumed competent unless proven otherwise. Under a traditional tenure system, the employee must demonstrate worthiness for tenure during the probationary period. Not unexpectedly, therefore, unions concentrate on developing elaborate criteria and procedures the institution must use to prove an individual does not deserve to be retained; tenure systems, on the other hand, focus principally upon criteria the candidate must satisfy to merit tenure and only secondarily upon general criteria that should be applied to detenure someone.

The same institutions and faculty that turn to collective negotiations for economic security may also turn to unions for assurances of academic freedom. Lower-tier institutions have historically been more vulnerable to attacks on academic freedom. Financial dependency and lack of strong traditions have weakened the ability of these schools to withstand and repel such attacks. In addition, attacks on academic freedom have succeeded because academic freedom has never been fully defined. Unions propose, at least implicitly, to remedy this situation by developing a comprehensive definition of academic freedom that protects all unit members, not merely the tenured faculty. The new rubric will be "terms and conditions of employment," a broad umbrella of protection. As terms and conditions of employment, what is taught, when, where, and how it is taught (all issues traditionally but vaguely encompassed by the term *academic freedom*) will become negotiable and, hence, contractual. As an element of a legal contract, these issues will be protected as never before and the protection will spread wider than ever before to all members of the bargaining unit.

[5] E. C. Ladd, Jr., and S. M. Lipset, *Professors, Unions, and American Higher Education* (Washington, D.C.: American Enterprise Institute, 1973).
[6] *The Chronicle of Higher Education,* November 26, 1973, p. 8.

While affirmative action and unionization both threaten traditional tenure systems, the two forces are by no means entirely compatible themselves. For example, the differences between tenure quotas and affirmative-action plans are not that substantial; both programs strive to manage personnel so as to assure flexibility necessary to allow germane and diverse appointments. If faculty unions successfully argue that tenure quota policies are terms and conditions of employment, a matter now hotly debated but not settled, then it would seem but a small step to assert that affirmative action goals and timetables are also negotiable. After all, affirmative-action plans affect appointment and reappointment decisions perhaps as much as tenure.

Suppose affirmative-action goals are subject to negotiation. Even with the best intentions presumed, it would be difficult to foresee a union arguing for more turnover and more nonretentions to increase the opportunities for management to appoint more women and minority-group members. The unions are more likely to argue for other solutions, such as a lower faculty-student ratio or the addition of more students to generate additional faculty positions. While these solutions would certainly benefit affirmative action, few campus observers would agree that these proposals represent realistic alternatives. In fact, for affirmative-action officers the dilemma seems to be how to add minorities and women as student-teacher ratios rise and the pool of available students shrinks.

Where new faculty slots do exist, unionized schools may be disadvantaged at the marketplace. Teacher unions have historically supported fixed pay scales, the so-called *lockstep system*. Allegedly, lockstep systems, based upon objective criteria such as length of service and academic credentials, bar. or at least limit administrators from offering different salaries to equally qualified employees for reasons such as favoritism. In the realities of the marketplace, however, the lockstep system remains the pursuit of affirmative-action objectives. Since the demand for affirmative-action appointments exceeds the supply, the market price for minorities and women frequently exceeds the salary level necessary to attract comparable male Caucasians. Yet a lockstep system will be unable to accommodate that reality since it prohibits salary disparities except those based upon seniority or academic credentials. For example, the contract negotiated between the State of New Jersey and the New Jersey State Federation of Teachers (A.F.T., A.F.L.-C.I.O.) bars the state colleges from hiring at the assistant-professor level unless the person possesses the appropriate termi-

nal degree or has completed all the requirements for the degree with
the exception of the dissertation. Unable to pay the necessary premium
to hire qualified minorities and women, unionized schools will lose
these candidates to campuses that retain the flexibility to grapple with
the marketplace. Incidentally, the Equal Work, Equal Pay Act also
appears to prohibit premium payments for reasons related to race or
sex. To date, however, the practice of premium payments has not been
tested as a violation of the Equal Pay Act.

Finally, to the extent that union contracts replace tenure systems as the primary basis for employment security, conflict with affirmative-action regulations will arise. With negotiated agreements as the
cornerstone for job security, seniority will certainly be cited as the
fundamental principle governing an employee's hold on a position.
However, most minorities and women have only recently been appointed to faculty rank. If retrenchment and related cutbacks lead to
layoffs, a circumstance that has already descended on several campuses
both large and small, the newer appointees will be among the earliest
casualties. In short, minorities and women will face an all too familiar
condition—the last hired will be the first fired, unless affirmative action
prevails.

What will ensue when affirmative action, unionization and
tenure collide? There are some clear signals. As construed by the Supreme Court in the *Griggs* case, the Civil Rights Act provides that
"practices, procedures, or tests neutral on their face and even neutral
in terms of intent, cannot be maintained if they operate to 'freeze'
the *status quo* of prior discriminatory employment practices." Even the
Nixon administration, not a noted advocate of civil rights, recently
determined that long-established policies that produced and maintained employment discrimination must be abandoned. In a January,
1973, directive, James Hodgson, then Secretary of Labor, commanded
the Bethlehem Steel plant at Sparrows Point, Maryland, "to correct
a seniority system that has been found to perpetuate the effects of past
discrimination in the assignment of blacks to jobs in departments
with limited advancement opportunities."[7] Hodgson so ruled because
the seniority system of the company locked blacks into inferior positions. As authority to act, Hodgson cited Executive Order 11246, the
same order that governs affirmative action for colleges and universities.

The parallels surely strike close to the campus. Tenure to a

[7] "Bethelehem Steel Required to Bar Racial Inequities," *The New
York Times,* January 1, 1973, pp. 1–12.

significant degree freezes the existing system, thereby limiting opportunities for employment. Tenure also locks minority-group members and women into junior positions, thus curtailing opportunities for advancement. In fact, should tenure quotas or limits gain additional support in the academic community, the lockout from senior tenured positions will become even more severe. And should more faculties unionize and accept a traditional labor role, the courts as well as the state and federal governments will be more apt to regard tenure as a seniority system designed to enhance job security. To the degree that tenure practices and union seniority systems discriminate against minorities and women, external authorities will undoubtedly intervene and order the practices and systems revised or even eliminated.

In sum, affirmative action and unionization are likely to force an end to current tenure practices. And where affirmative action conflicts with unionization, federal and state agencies will hold for affirmative action.

Impact of Collective Bargaining on Students

Linda Bond

The "boom and quasi bust" of higher education in the sixties and seventies has had its impact on college faculties. Arguments favoring faculty unionism gain a sense of immediacy as student enrollments decline and state appropriations for higher education level off in the wake of inflation and shifting priorities. The move to extend collective-bargaining rights to public employees in general has placed pressure on faculty members in state-supported institutions. Many people are going for the public pie; faculty members feel forced to unionize just to keep their piece.

Almost three hundred colleges and universities bargained collectively with representatives of their faculties last year. Bargaining units represent about eighty thousand faculty members, roughly 15 percent of the national teaching strength. In late 1969, only twenty-seven contracts had been negotiated; 156 are in force today. Today, collective bargaining in higher education is primarily a community-college phenomenon. Union activity has not matched the early predictions of very rapid growth, and the level of activity is not constant. The trend, however, is ever upward. The future of faculty unionization lies in large part with the success of state legislative activity. Twenty-nine states have not yet passed enabling legislation covering academic collective bargaining. Of these twenty-nine, however, legislation enabling faculty collective bargaining is under consideration in all but one state. When and if such legislation is successful, faculty unionization will without a doubt greatly accelerate.

Student concern regarding faculty unionism does not stem from a belief that public-employee collective bargaining is bad public policy. To the contrary, most students recognize the civil rights issue involved. Our concern stems from the impact that collective bargaining has had, and will have, on the quality of university instruction and the participation of students in university governance. Students are concerned that increases in salaries and fringe benefits won by faculty unions will come out of students' pockets in the form of higher tuition. At a time when state dollars for higher education are being held constant, students are the most politically convenient source of increased revenues. Students fear that faculty strikes will interrupt their education and that faculty collective bargaining will freeze students out of their hard-won participation in campus decisionmaking. Most important, students are concerned that the quality of the educational product will be eroded.

These are legitimate concerns. In the industrial model, collective bargaining is a bilateral (union-management) negotiating process that traditionally takes place in secret. The lines between faculty and administration (union-management) are very uncertain, particularly in institutions where faculty have a high degree of control over their working environment. Education is a process, not a product which can be seen in terms of a producer-consumer model. In spite of the differences between education and industry, most colleges have adopted the industrial model and its terminology. "Conditions of employment" in the education contract involve educational policy issues by definition. "Wages, hours, and working conditions" are being interpreted to include questions of class size, faculty workload, curriculum, tenure, and research. Stipulations regarding teacher and course evaluations have been included in almost every contract now binding. It is not unusual for questions concerning access to student records, the academic calendar, and the administration of student services to be rigidly defined in a negotiated contract.

Faculty contract demands unquestionably have gone beyond economic issues. Two colleges in Massachusetts, for example, have placed their entire governance plans in their collectively bargained contracts. Campus governance structures, once flexible enough to accommodate student involvement, are superseded by newly created joint administrative-faculty advisory committees rigidly defined by law. Educational policy issues are negotiated in secret behind closed doors. Course offerings may be reduced or entire programs phased out. Innovative educational programs that make use of community resources may be eliminated due to rigid definitions of faculty workload. Remedial and other support programs for minority students may well be the first to go because they add to faculty workload. Student needs for part-time learning opportunities on evenings and weekends conflict with faculty desires for more regular hours. Student-controlled courses and evaluations of their teachers are victims of faculty desires to limit such judgments to their peers. "Due process" clauses, which call for automatic promotion regardless of merit, further decrease the impact of evaluative mechanisms.

These are all educational policy questions of vital concern to students, yet students are not at the table when they are being negotiated. Students in the Chicago Community College system (1968), the City University of New York (1973), the State University of New York (1972), and Michigan State University (1972) were virtually excluded from participation or consultation once contracts began to be negotiated. Out of sight and thus out of mind, students and their interests in educational policy remain either unknown or ignored.

Unfortunately, it appears that the faculty perceive their negotiating rights under collective bargaining in the climate of collective bargaining in private industry. When issues concerning campus governance arise the faculty see the maintenance or improvement of the rights and benefits stipulated in their contract as their major priority.[1] Put simply, the situation can be interpreted as faculty power versus student power. Still smarting from the gains students made in the 1960s in the areas of curriculum and faculty review and promotion, professors seek to reassert their prerogatives through the negotiating process. If the growth of faculty collective bargaining is inevitable, as many analysts predict, and if the scope of issues negotiated behind closed doors continues to expand, as it no doubt will given political realities, students must involve themselves in the bargaining process or forfeit their role in university decisionmaking.

How can student involvement best be accomplished? Several strategies have emerged: to ask for judicial intervention in the event of a faculty strike, to seek observer status at the negotiations, to seek participatory status in the bargaining between faculty and administration, to establish limited tripartite bargaining through legislation that would limit the issues on which students could participate and exercise a veto, to gain full tripartite bargaining through lobbying for legislation that would protect student interests.[2] Judicial intervention is not particularly attractive; strikes at educational institutions are not generally resolved through injunctions; student participation cannot be gained through the courts. Seemingly, the only way that student participation can be ensured is by so stipulating in the enabling legislation as it is being written. All other roads to student involvement are less satisfactory, for they depend on the permission of the other parties.

Full tripartite bargaining, allowing students to sit in on all bargaining sessions with full rights to information and the right to veto proposed agreements, is probably not politically feasible at this time. That student lobbies are presenting this tripartite plan as a model, however, forces state legislators to recognize the inter-relation of all negotiable issues and their impact on student rights and educational quality. Providing for student observer status is feasible and has been done. In California, for example, the proposed legislation was amended to allow for student observers. The bill was later vetoed by Governor Reagan, and student lobbyists, believing the amendment was too weak, joined those asking for the veto.

Students should not be content with observer status as their

[1] Alan R. Shark, "The Students' Right to Collective Bargaining," *Change Magazine,* April 1973, p. 9.

[2] I am in debt to Kevin Bacon, Co-Director of the U.C. Student Lobby, for his help in writing this section on possible student strategies.

goal. We should be able to lobby for a provision in the legislation that will allow students to sit in on all negotiating sessions, with the right to participate in discussions, be represented by counsel, and the right to caucus. We might identify those issues over which students could, as provided by statute, exercise a veto power. These might include the place of student-conducted evaluation of teaching in the faculty promotion and review process, student participation in academic senate committees, the student role in academic planning and curriculum review processes, class size and the diversity and frequency of course offerings, grading policy, policies concerning student-faculty grievances, student disciplinary procedures, allocation of income from student fees, and provisions affecting the operation, financing, staffing, and management of student services. The law could also require an educational-impact report from each group participating in the negotiations. The report would cover the impact of the proposed agreement on educational quality, the level of service to students, and the increased costs to students.

Needless to say, strategies that involve influencing the shape and scope of the enabling legislation presuppose a permanent well-financed, full-time staff at the state capitol responsible to chosen student representatives. The spontaneous, haphazard efforts by students to influence governmental policy in the sixties were largely ineffective. Lobbying for provisions in legislation to protect student interests in academic collective bargaining will necessitate responsibility, permanence, and a sense of history. These elements are present in the state-wide student lobby in California; they can become part of student organizations in other states as well.

Aggressive and external student strategies would not be necessary if policymakers in the university and legislature would draw distinctions between collective bargaining in private industry and public service, and among institutions within the public-service category. Industrial employer-employee and producer-consumer models simply do not fit four-year higher educational institutions, in spite of any characteristics they may be coming to share with the American factory. The argument can be made, for example, that students are not only the consumers of higher education, but its coproducers as well.

❧ 21 ❧

Collective Bargaining and Policymaking

Neil S. Bucklew

A̲lthough the phenomenon of academic collective bargaining is relatively new, distinct models have developed. These models reflect a range of responses to a central dilemma—how does a university employ the new decisionmaking process of bargaining in the context of a multiparty governance that in large measure is a consensus system? This question can be paraphrased in labor-relations terms: What is the appropriate scope of bargaining?

Three basic patterns of negotiations have evolved during the brief history of faculty collective bargaining in institutions of higher education. The first may be described as *comprehensive negotiations*. In this pattern, the parties negotiate over a broad range of subjects that include wage and fringe items as well as professional items such as work load, class size, academic personnel issues, teaching effectiveness, and calendar. The resulting contract describes these matters in both policy and procedural terms. The second pattern is *structural negotiations*. In this type, the parties deal with the broad range of topics but tend to use "constitutional" language to describe professional and governance matters. For example, tenure may be described by reference to the decisionmaking hierarchy and timetable used but there would be no description of policies or criteria. The third bargaining pattern is *employment negotiations*. In this case, the parties may discuss a full range of topics but the contract is basically limited to employment issues such as wages, fringe benefits, leaves, working conditions. In this pattern there tends to be no contractual reference to governance or professional issues.

By analyzing the rationales undergirding these differing patterns, we should be able to get some idea of their potential impact on academic decisionmaking. I would like to identify first the arguments supporting some combination of the *comprehensive* and *structural negotiations*. The rationales for each are similar, and in practice the two approaches are often linked together. Both are broad-scale negotiations, and the arguments presented in their support come from traditional campus experiences and from such external influences as industrial labor relations and the labor law.

In *comprehensive* or *structural negotiations,* as in all negotiations, the faculty of the university choose the union as their exclusive bargaining agent. The faculty intends to substitute a new and different decisionmaking system for the historical governance structure of the university. The total range of subjects—from wages and fringe benefits to governance systems—are appropriate for negotiations. Both parties may decide that a matter should not be contractual; any such decisions should be made at the bargaining table and not by one of the parties unilaterally. Or the parties may decide that the present system is adequate. In that case, they could describe in constitutional terms the present system and give it the power of a contractual agreement.

The faculty is unlikely to ratify any agreement that limits their involvement in governing the university. Any attempt to limit the scope of negotiations so that issues of governance and academic personnel are excluded will lead to frustration and confrontation. This threat to collegiality must not be ignored. If the university administration refuses to deal with the union on all matters as an equal party, faculty members will become angry. Even if a limited bargaining posture on the part of the university is strategically possible, such a strategy will likely result in pitting faculty against faculty or faculty against students. For the same faculty members are represented by the traditional government system and collective bargaining. Their interests are the same under both structures. Collective bargaining simply represents an alternate way of resolving issues of concern to faculty members. Any attempt to limit negotiations is an attempt to limit the legal and appropriate role of the union. And any attempt to limit the legal and appropriate role of the union is an attempt to limit the appropriate and legal role of the faculty.

It is important to incorporate, at least in descriptive form, the basic processes of faculty involvement in governance. Even if the present structure is continued, these processes should be protected against unilateral change on the part of the university. Faculty inclusion in the collective bargaining agreement will mean that any change in current practice must be agreed to by the faculty representative. As part of a legally binding document, the faculty role in governance will have more than the voluntary status formerly enjoyed as board policy. In like manner, it is possible to describe governance processes by a collective-bargaining agreement in a way that protects the multiparty characteristics of governance within the university community. The appropriate involvement of students and other constituent groups can be acknowledged and even ratified by those constituencies (as in the Massachusetts State Colleges contracts).

In addition to covering the total range of issues that concern the faculty, *comprehensive negotiations* can include a description of the process to be used when established policies are reconsidered—for instance, when an established personnel policy is changed. By specifying the mechanisms for handling such matters, the contract can protect all parties from the ill effects of crisis decisionmaking, and policy changes can occur rationally.

The pattern of *employment negotiations* stands in contrast to the inclusive, broad-scale contracts resulting from *comprehensive* or *structural negotiations*. The arguments for adopting this limited system are based in large part on the character of faculty and the nature of academic decisionmaking. Collective bargaining has brought into sharp focus the dual roles played by faculty members in the modern university. On the one hand, faculty members serve as professionals with a crucial involvement in the development and execution of the instructional, research, and service functions of the university. They are responsible, with the university administration and others, for describing, defining, and implementing the purposes of the university. Academic programs, curriculum, peer review and appeal, and policies relating to professional status such as tenure and promotion are specific areas requiring this consultative process. The deliberative and consultative relationships inherent in these matters must be preserved and enhanced if the basic goals of the university are to be reached. On the other hand, in addition to their professional role, faculty members are also employees of the university and have an understandable concern for their personal welfare and financial interests. In the context of industrial bargaining, the matters usually discussed are wages, hours, and other terms and conditions of employment. In the academic context, these are also significant matters. But in addition to being an employee, the faculty member is a professional person with continuing interest and involvement in the governance of the university. The contract of faculty bargaining must reflect these dual faculty roles.

The *employment-negotiations* pattern offers, I believe, the best means of accomplishing this. First, it recognizes that the university is a unique system of shared responsibility. Many matters are deliberative in nature and the judgments are often a result of extensive analysis, consideration, and reconsideration. Academic decisions about tenure, promotion, reappointment, and curricular matters would be qualitatively inferior if they were placed in the bargaining context instead of the deliberative context. First, the parties would be forced to assume an adversarial posture instead of an open, deliberative role. Second, there would be no recognition of the multiple constituencies affected by decisions (faculty, administrators, students, public, staff employees), since collective bargaining is essentially a bipartite system. Third, the flexibility needed to resolve complex issues would be greatly reduced because decisions in collective bargaining are required by statute to be reduced to written form and placed in a legally binding document. When faculty choose a bargaining agent, they do not intend to diminish their professional responsibilities in the university community. To assume a collective-bargaining approach that is too inclusive would place in jeopardy their role in the established governance structure.

The negotiation and contractualization of governance and academic decisionmaking systems would also have the effect of changing the nature of these systems. Instead of being deliberate in nature and reflecting a commitment to peer evaluation, decisionmaking systems would become matters for contractual grievances. Defined as *allega-*

tions of contractual violations, contractual grievances are the method of assuring that the university interprets and applies the contract in an acceptable manner. If various management reviews do not resolve a grievance, it then is submitted to an outside third party or arbitrator for a final binding decision. This process is significantly different from traditional peer-review systems.

The tenure process can illustrate this. This process acknowledges the primary role of the academic unit to evaluate colleagues and recommend a tenure decision. When tenure is denied, the basic appeal mechanism available to the faculty member is a peer-review system. A hearing assures that proper procedures were followed and that error of fact, gross prejudice, capricious action, or factors that violate academic freedom did not influence the decision. The primary responsibility for review is in the hands of academic colleagues. If the process for making tenure decisions were contractualized, arbitration would be substituted for a peer-based review and the final decision would be in the hands of a third party who would provide an interpretation of a legally binding document. It is most likely that the burden of proof would shift from the nontenured faculty member making the appeal to the academic unit involved. The result could be "instant tenure."

The New York Times, in a December 6, 1972, editorial addressed to the issue of including tenure as a topic in faculty collective-bargaining agreements, said of the traditional peer-review approach, "This system is not without flaws. Like any such jury system, it is subject to human and professional misjudgments, and even to occasional abuse and injustice. But it has also given colleges and universities an extraordinary leverage on quality control—an essential counterbalance to the virtually ironclad job security that comes with tenure. To abandon this approach in favor of what would in effect be automatic promotion and instant tenure, with appeals ultimately left to outside arbitrators, would seriously undercut the role of academic self-government. In plain language, it would mean adoption of the public school staffing model under which all certified teachers are essentially interchangeable parts. It is a model ill-suited to the maintenance of high scholarly standards in universities."

To negotiate within an area where the issues to be resolved and contractualized are either undefined or broadly defined will only enhance the possibility of conflict. In particular, it will lead to jurisdictional conflicts between the bargaining agent and such established forms of faculty governance as the academic council or senate. An inherent tension arises when a bargaining agent coexists with a senate. The university administration is in a unique position to influence the jurisdictions of these groups. If the bargaining agent is not to invade the appropriate jurisdiction of the senate and vice versa, the administration will have to espouse a clear concept of their appropriate roles.

The possible erosion of jurisdiction has been succinctly described by Ralph Browne[1]: "Once a bargaining agent has the weight of statutory certification behind him, a familiar process comes into play. First, the matter of salaries is linked to workload; workload is then directly related to class size; class size to range of offerings and range of offerings to curricular policy. Dispute over class size may also lead to bargaining over admissions policies." An articulated limitation to bargaining issues would keep such overlaps of jurisdiction from occurring, and that is the kind of limitation the *employment negotiations* model provides. It is concerned with the issues of wages, fringe benefits, and directly related conditions of employment. Collective-bargaining tradition has shown that these types of special-interest issues, in which the parties tend to assume an adversarial posture, have been satisfactorily resolved at the bargaining table. And there is evidence in the limited negotiations to date in higher education that faculty have found the collective-bargaining process an adequate way to resolve such fiscal issues in the academic world.

Collective bargaining is here. It will be adopted in a growing number of colleges and universities and has proved its viability in industry. Whether collective bargaining will be practiced on campuses in a manner that is responsive to the unique characteristics of academic policymaking remains to be seen.

[1] Ralph Browne, "Collective Bargaining in Higher Education," *University of Michigan Law Review,* March 1969, p. 1075.

Alternative to Tenure

Myron J. Lunine

Hampshire College is nearing its twentieth year of plan-
ning efforts and finishing its fourth year with a steady-state student body
of 1,250 in residence, two hundred fifty on leave, and a faculty of one
hundred twenty-five persons occupying about eighty FTE's—all living
and working within the viable Five College Consortium.

Hampshire is actively involved in a number of experiments.
The first—and this order is not one of priority or sequence necessarily
—is a financial experiment. We are attempting to be a private, high-
quality, experimental liberal-arts college that derives all its operating
budget from fees. This effort necessitates a sixteen to one student-faculty ratio and a ratio of one full professor to two associate professors
and four assistant professors. Our second experiment is in governance.

We are attempting to diffuse power, decentralize authority, share responsibility, and maximize participation. As a result, the administration has some of the best and worst features of Periclean Athens, the Byzantine Empire, the Federalist Papers, early Adam Smith, late Rousseau, Proudhon, and Mao Tse-tung. Our third experiment is an effort at building community, individual, and corporate citizenship. Our fourth experiment is cooperation with the four institutions that actually spawned us—Smith, Mount Holyoke, Amherst, and the University of Massachusetts. These colleges work with us in a coordinated, complementary, and reciprocal way.

Our fifth and sixth experiments are more at the heart of the educational venture itself. These experiments restructure the academic organization to mesh the operations of four multidisciplinary schools with cross-school appointments and programs, and the very central experiment of redefining and assessing educational progress by examinations at three consecutive divisional levels—a process that takes the place of grades, credit hours, and class standing. These last two experiments give us an educational way of life in which each student enjoys (or endures) self-defined, self-paced, self-placed programs of learning.

The implications of this educational way of life are far-reaching indeed for the teacher. The teacher's role at Hampshire is more facilitative than didactic, more advisory than directive; it is richly infused with diverse pedagogical and convivial interactions. The teacher's role is greatly varied and seeks to respond to each student's needs, interests, and possibilities. The faculty load is heavy (in both senses of the word).

Hampshire uses a renewable contract plan in the belief that traditional life-tenure systems do not necessarily encourage continuing professional self-examination or evaluation by one's own peers and students. Nor do they necessarily encourage pedagogical experiment, development, and renewal. Nor are life-tenure systems necessarily the only way to insure academic freedom and professional dignity. (In a letter to Hampshire College in 1971, the American Association of University Professors stated that "Academic freedom and tenure are inseparable principles." I sincerely hope not, for academic freedom is too precious a fruit to grow on only one tree—especially in this period of pruning.) Stated more positively, the periodic evaluation of faculty effectiveness in the Hampshire reappointment process is to insure sustained quality among faculty. Career development is encouraged among faculty, who will be asked periodically to submit new proposals for their next contract term. The college can continue to carry on experimental efforts by having an opportunity to discontinue faculty no longer committed to the major mission of the college, and the college is commited to developing new career opportunities for departing faculty.

These positive approaches are yet to be validated; the college has done better anticipating the problems. Hampshire is discovering, for example, that agreed definitions underlying judgmental decisions and evaluative procedures having high consensual endorsement are very difficult to achieve. And the college is concerned that peer evaluation across all ranks (in the absence of a tenured senior faculty) and student participation (in view of personalized, if not intimate, faculty-student relationships) might lead to a lowering of standards.

The Hampshire policy, formally adopted in 1971 and recently reaffirmed, generally is to appoint faculty for four years under a renewable contract plan rather than follow the procedures set down in the 1940 Statement on Academic Freedom and Tenure, procedures followed at the majority of institutions. The college does, of course, endorse the Statement on Academic Freedom and is rigorous in safeguarding such freedom. But instead of a single tenure decision, the Hampshire reappointment process uses renewable three- to seven-year contracts, subject to annual reviews by the school dean and a thorough evaluation completed seventeen months before termination of the contract. This evaluation for reappointment is initiated by the dean of the college and conducted by the school to which the faculty member is assigned. The review mechanism is a college committee consisting of the president, the college dean, five elected faculty, and two elected students, all of whom have roles and responsibilities to deal expeditiously and judiciously with crucial and sometimes confidential materials. The first appointment and all reappointments are based on professional competence and promise as a *teacher* (in many kinds of faculty-student transactions), as a *scholar* (public or private research; artistry; craftsmanship; evidence of scholarly, artistic, or pedagogical productivity), and as a *contributor* to the life and well-being of the college, the consortium, or the wider community.

Of sixty-three faculty members up for reappointment in the past four years, two were turned down by the College Committee on Faculty Reappointments, with the president upholding one of those decisions, and two who were recommended for reappointment by the committee were turned down by the president. The results are three non-reappointments out of sixty-three, with one of the three now appealing his case. Such numbers bear a great deal of scrutiny and explication. They leave many problems unsolved: diverse definitions of *good* (good teaching, good advising); inconsistency of procedures and inadequacy or unevenness of materials at each level and during each phase of the process; the bias of data generated only for the reappointment process; the reappointment process becoming the preoccupation of too many faculty—with the possible consequences of anxiety and conformism; and the reappointment syndrome ironically discouraging daring, adventurous, fruitful pedagogical failures.

On the positive side, the college is moving toward more consistent values, definitions, and procedures; greater sophistication and professionalism in evaluating teaching and advising; and an increased awareness on the part of virtually everyone at the college of the complexity, fragility, and worth of what we are trying to do. For what we are trying to do is to create a mentality and construct an instrumentality that will accomplish the following: insure the faculty of academic freedom, professional dignity, just rewards, and reasonable job security; insure that students will have a quality faculty and a real role to play in faculty evaluation; serve the interests of Hampshire College with respect to faculty renewal (in both senses), improvement of evaluation systems, and participation by all members of the community; and serve, in a small way, as a pertinent pilot effort or model for other institutions.

Will the Hampshire contract plan succeed? In playing prophet, or at least predictor, one must take into account the general return to educational orthodoxy, the anti-intellectualism and genuine economic constraints that affect and afflict the academy and the academic marketplace, the possible impact on tenure systems and on contract systems of collective bargaining, and the condition and direction of the half-dozen other Hampshire College experiments. For me, the real question is not whether our present problems (diversity of definitions, inconsistency of practices, intrusion of personalities and politics) preclude accomplishing the purposes of our contract system. Nor is the question whether this difficult and demanding contract system itself helps develop a culture and an environment appropriate and conducive to the humane and efficient functioning of the contract system.

The question is how do we understand and manage processes that are both the means and the ends of rational and compassionate institutions and of academically free and educationally responsible individuals?

$\mathcal{Z}23\mathcal{Z}$

New Life for Faculty
and Institutions

James L. Bess

$\mathcal{Z}\mathcal{Z}\mathcal{Z}\mathcal{Z}\mathcal{Z}\mathcal{Z}\mathcal{Z}\mathcal{Z}\mathcal{Z}\mathcal{Z}$

There has been much talk lately of eliminating tenure, firing faculty outright, increasing faculty workloads, and prescribing faculty activities in greater detail to make them more efficient. Within our institutions of higher education, typical responses to these pressures are defensive and fear-ridden. Collective bargaining and other devices have been established to ensure that existing practices are not disturbed. The stage is set for a battle among faculty, administrators, and fund sources in which there can be few winners. For if to knuckle under to externally imposed standards is educationally and institutionally disastrous, perpetuation of present conditions in the academic profession is hardly any better.

Any answer to this dilemma must include a recognition of three systematically related areas in American society—our culture, its institutions of higher education, and the academic profession. These problems overlap, and workable solutions to them must be integrated. New modes of interaction are needed between academic personnel and community, removing barriers to the flow of information and ideas. There must be new conditions within institutions, integrating faculty and institutional goals, as person and organization are united in synergistic efforts. And there need to be revitalized modes of interaction between the institutions and the culture, reaffirming the role of higher education as a moral force and precursor of change in society.

The basic question is what fundamental changes within our institutions of higher education can affect culture, institution, and individual at the same time? One response lies in the considerable strengthening of the public-service mission of our colleges and universities. The creation of strong separate units of public service within each institution would provide unique opportunities for faculty to move into new roles. Public-service roles would permit faculty to move gracefully out of traditional teaching and research roles and gradually, if desired, out of the academic profession. Such activity would provide institutions with formal organizational structures to accommodate the changing needs of its workers. Units of public service would permit the institution to take on a more direct stance in addressing the practical needs of the society and in enriching its culture. By making institutions more valuable to the surrounding social system, higher education would become more visibly productive, increasing the probability of greater financial and moral support.

Many faculty may be psychologically predisposed to make the kind of changes implied here for several reasons. A number of faculty, young and old, partly through poor advice, have entered the academic profession for the wrong reasons. Some of these faculty may have discovered the error in their vocational choice while quite young, others not until later; but both age groups often feel condemned to continue in an occupation for which they are ill-suited and which they presently find distasteful. They may also resent being confined to a single institution in these times of severely reduced occupational mobility.

Other faculty are simply tired. They have been teaching for twenty to twenty-five years and have grown bored with the repetition of activity; even exceptional teachers experience this ennui. Many faculty also may have already made their most creative research contributions but continue to do research because that role is virtually the only one they have been trained to perform. At mid-career, these teachers have come to understand the limitations of their professional capacities and they are aware that their lack of certain critical skills may hinder their future achievements and career progress. They begin to question their identities and self-concepts, wondering if their views of themselves are valid and whether and how they might change in the future. These faculty are increasingly beset by loss of confidence and insecurity.

Such anxieties might cause adults to be defensive, rigid, and protective of what remains of their relatively more precarious egos and sense of competence. Yet it is possible to conceive of work and family conditions in which such fears could make them more open to alternatives in their lives and more receptive to new solutions and perceived problems. Clearly, these solutions must appear challenging but not overly threatening. They must also take cognizance of certain developmental changes at mid-life that are of a positive nature.[1]

If faculty are offered real alternatives to their present career tracks, some, if not many, will be interested in and willing to change roles. Their new organizational homes cannot, however, be a kind of elephant burial grounds where psychologically moribund faculty go to die. Fortunately, an enormous number of opportunities exist for faculty both out of the academic world and within it. The problem is how to make these opportunities known to faculty and the movement into them sufficiently stable and smooth to override the threat that significant change in life always presents.

The advantages of a transitional staging area such as that offered by separate and well funded public-service units suggest themselves strongly in answer to this dilemma. Such an organizational entity meets the needs of the institution by making the institution more valuable to the constituencies that support it. This organizational entity would permit the transfer from overstaffed departments of those faculty ready to embark on a new career, thus freeing the academic marketplace and making room for younger persons in the profession. And such public-service units would provide a new and vital moral

---

[1] Compare E. H. Erikson, *Childhood and Society* (New York: W. W. Norton Co., 1963); R. L. White, *Lives in Progress* (New York: Holt, Rinehart and Winston, 1952); M. E. Linden and D. Courtney, "The Human Life Cycle and Its Interruptions," *American Journal of Psychiatry*, 1953, Vol. 109.

force, infusing the culture with collaborative modes of work. It is easy to envision a public-service unit with many of the same structural characteristics as the county agricultural agencies in the period following the Morrill Act. Public-service extension agents could provide needed services to business, hospitals, municipal governments, welfare agencies, and individuals. The newest information produced by research could be made readily available to those in need. The humanities are by no means to be left out of this model. One can picture free concerts, painting workshops, and lectures on literature emanating from colleges and universities.

The idea of public service is not new to higher education; faculty have been engaged in it for many years. What is new is the formal institutionalization of public service—the establishment and full staffing of an organizational unit within the college or university for the express purpose of providing services to society. Faculty seeking respite from traditional teaching or research roles would look to the public-service unit as a way station to careers outside or as a career possibility in itself. From the security of academia, they could explore opportunities outside. With a familiar home base and an accustomed social status, faculty would feel free to explore new and different talents and interests—indeed, to experiment with dormant parts of themselves that could provide more mid-life satisfaction than the ritualistic performance of roles which may have become boring and repetitious.

But even if outside opportunities are available and a new structure has been set up within higher education, other inducements will be necessary to encourage faculty to make career shifts. The way vertical and horizontal transfers are handled in industrial organizations unfortunately provides little guidance here. Typically, nonacademic organizations are concerned with minimizing the disruption to the flow of work and to the existing social structure. The orientation is toward using workers whose contributions have been less than optimum in ways which primarily serve the organization, with little care for individual satisfaction and continued personal growth. Goode notes:

[The question is what to do] with that inevitable segment of a group that is relatively less productive or competent. How can the group utilize them, how gain from them that smaller, but measurable amount of marginal productivity the group believes their effort can can contribute.

More generally, given the existence of the relatively inept in nearly all groups, what are the patterns or process which on the one hand will protect them from the rigors of untrammeled competition (and thus gain their support and contribution) and on the other hand protect the group from the potentially destructive consequences of their ineptitude. Needless to say, there is no evidence that the social arrangements now observable are the most productive possible, whether of material goods or human satisfaction.[2]

Happily we do know something about how shifts from position or status can be made more attractive. Strauss suggests that when the movement in organizations is regularized and highly institutionalized, the person shifting is prepared for the next step, is forewarned about what will be expected of him, and can adjust himself psychologically. This is especially true when "the institution stands ready with devices to make him forget, to plunge him into the new office, to point out and allow him to experience the gratifications accruing to it, as well as to force him to abandon the old."[3] Transitions should be scheduled and governed by clear rules. The rules should contain a prescribed series of steps that a person must go through to complete the passage, and they should have regularized actions which must be carried out by the participants in order to insure that the passage has been completed.[4] Ambiguities in the mode of change itself or in the nature of the new job requirements must be avoided.

Beside the formal institutional devices for making the transition more attractive, other devices may be needed to aid the faculty member during the initial period in his new position. Goffman in a landmark article gives some insight in this area. He suggests that it is necessary in the case of an individual who has been conned for someone else to help reduce his anger so that the injury done to self-image can be repaired. "For the mark, cooling represents a process of an adjustment to an impossible situation—a situation arising from having defined himself in a way which the social facts come to contradict. The mark must therefore be supplied with a new set of apologies for himself, a new framework in which to see himself and judge himself. A process of redefining himself along defensible lines must be instigated and

[2] W. J. Goode, "The Protection of the Inept," *American Sociological Review*, February 1967, *32*(1).

[3] Anselm L. Strauss, *Mirrors and Masks, The Search for Identity* (San Francisco: The Sociology Press, 1969), p. 104.

[4] Anselm L. Strauss, "Some Neglected Properties of Status Passage." In Howard S. Becker and associates (Eds.), *Institutions and the Person* (Chicago: Aldine Publishing Company, 1968), pp. 265–271.

carried along; since the mark himself is frequently in too weakened a condition to do this, the cooler must initially do it for him."[5]

While a faculty member moving to a public-service role is usually not considered a "mark"—that is, taken advantage of by the institution—some parallels are evident. Formal and informal "coolers," as Goffman calls them, would certainly be helpful in providing emotional support. There are at least three kinds of coolers who could perform this task: faculty spouses, institutional career counselors for faculty, and high-status informal leaders. In any faculty shift in status, it is suggested that each of these coolers know thoroughly the specific problems of personal change and the art of giving assistance.

What kinds of faculty are likely to take a chance on a new kind of public service unit within a college or university—and what kinds are needed? Clearly, to avoid being labeled a *department of failures,* the unit has to attract capable and respected people. If some of the best teachers and researchers can be induced to join the public-service unit initially, it will have a better chance of succeeding. A mode of recruitment and selection similar to that operating in departments will insure an aura of selectivity and respectability for the new unit. So also will formal leadership by a person with vice-presidential status, power, and responsibility.

In addition to good staffing, the public service unit will need an adequate budget to be effective. We should remember that since no new faculty would be added to the college or university, the total institutional budget is not likely to be increased materially. Also, legislatures and other sources of funds might be more inclined to support operations, the functions of which have been clearly differentiated, particularly if the teaching function was alleged to be overbudgeted (that is, overstaffed). In the long run, experiments with other forms of financing faculty in new career excursions can be integrated into the plan discussed here.[6]

Bell has warned that in a postindustrial society, the gap between social structure and culture will probably widen. "The lack of a rooted moral belief system is the cultural contradiction of the society, the deepest challenge to its survival. The post industrial society is a crescive, unplanned change in the character of society, the work-

[5] Irving Goffman, "On Cooling the Mark Out: Some Aspects of Adaptation to Failure," *Psychiatry,* November 1952, *15*(4).

[6] Carnegie Commission, *Toward a Learning Society* (New York: McGraw-Hill, 1973).

ing out of the logic of socioeconomic organization, and a change in the character of knowledge. At some point, the major social groups in society become conscious of the underlying social transformation and have to decide, politically, whether to accept the drift, accelerate it, impede it, or change its direction."[7]

Colleges and universities represent the greatest potential for meeting the challenge of providing a rooted moral belief system. Through their efforts in public service to revive a sagging society, colleges and universities can reinstill belief in the possibilities of social change for a better world. Furthermore, by providing a new and exemplary organizational model to permit individuals continued growth and development in their careers, higher education can demonstrate and experiment with life and work modes which are appropriate for the future.

[7] Daniel Bell, *The Coming of Post Industrial Society*, New York: Basic Books, Inc., 1973.

Policy Proposals
for Financing

G. Ben Lawrence

J ust as this nation began to demonstrate its commitment to equality of access to postsecondary education, the financial crisis of the late 1960s and early 1970s stalled those efforts. A major question in adjusting financial policies to new realities is how to finance continued efforts to provide postsecondary education for the poor and the minorities, still significantly underrepresented.

Convinced that additional public funds will not, or should not, become available to postsecondary education, some educators have proposed increasing tuition in public institutions so that middle- and upper-income families share the cost of achieving equality. The savings to public subsidy realized through increasing tuition would be dedicated to student financial assistance. In this way, the states would join with the federal government in a continuing effort to bring about equality of access. The economic evidence I have studied suggests that this plan would work quite well, with the proviso that state government dedicate the tuition revenue gained to financial aid for students in low-income categories.

Nevertheless, I do not concur with the proposal to increase tuition, not only as a matter of principle, but also on pragmatic grounds. Increasing tuition to provide student financial aid to the poor places a burden of wealth redistribution only on those who receive postsecondary education benefits. Redistribution of wealth should really belong to the whole of society. No matter what the disposition of the increased revenue, increased tuition at public institutions will cause 1 percent to 3 percent of all students from middle-income families to drop out for every $100 increase in tuition, depending on the student's level and type of institution attended. Those students who choose to remain in college must place increased financial burdens on their families, already strapped by financial pressures in an erratic economy, or the students will have to change their standard of living dramatically while in college.

If we are proposing policy to redistribute wealth, it should be done through tax policy and not through educational financing policy. Low tuition in public institutions has been developed as a matter of public policy from the conviction that the social benefits of postsecondary education justify such subsidy. I see no strong or persistent evidence that this policy should be changed. On the contrary, societal expectations of the general educational and skill levels of adults have increased to the point where general access to two years of postsecondary education has become more a societal obligation than an avenue to individual opportunity. Thus, continued general public subsidy is justified and perhaps should be increased. Tuition levels should be set low enough to assure that the majority of students can have access to public institutions without need for public assistance.

I must note, however, that while my preferences are to the contrary, the economics of the situation suggest that tuitions at the upper division and graduate levels may have to rise to bring in sufficient revenue. The justification for choosing these levels, while harsh, is that current manpower projections suggest a high probability of underemployment, if not unemployment, for people with baccalaureate, advanced professional, and graduate degrees. To some extent this already has occurred, and society has somewhat less motivation to finance these levels through general subsidies. At the same time, an individual should have the opportunity to seek such degrees if he is capable, and is willing to bear some of the increased costs or able to obtain financial assistance based on merit or financial need.

Finally, I am not convinced that state legislatures generally would allocate increased tuition revenue to student financial assistance. If not, the result would mean not only that the inequities of student access would continue, but also that a reduction of middle-class enrollments would lead to even less overall revenue.

Equality of access is a social concern of high national priority and should be addressed by federal initiatives. The federal government should promote equality of access to postsecondary education through work-study programs and grants and loans to students and institutions. The government should enable both full-time and part-time students from low-income and middle-income families to enroll in and complete appropriate postsecondary-education programs. The Basic Educational Opportunity Grants program, if fully funded, would be an effective vehicle for promoting equal access.

The evidence suggests that low income is not the only, or even. the greatest, deterrent to equality of access. Family background and the choice of high school curriculum are more significant. I suggest, therefore, supplementing direct student grants with grants to institutions, in amounts determined by the income level of the student grant recipients. I believe that would provide the incentive and the resources for institutions to overcome nonfinancial barriers to equality of access. For example, I would recommend for each BEOG recipient from families with incomes under $5,000 a supplemental grant of $200; under $10,000, a supplemental grant of $100; under $15,000 a supplemental grant of $50; under $20,000, a supplemental grant of $25.

An especially aggressive policy toward equality of access might tie large institutional grants to students by income level, with the understanding that institutions could use some of the funds for student financial assistance. Such a policy would be more effective in motivating institutions to recruit, admit, and provide special services to low-income students than would a combination of direct student assistance and supplemental grants to institutions. The policy has the disadvantage, however, that institutions might not necessarily treat students with equal financial need in an equitable way.

The guaranteed student-loan program should be streamlined administratively and altered to remove the financial-needs test for adjusted family income at levels $18,000 and less. The program should provide interest subsidy during enrollment on loans to all students from families with adjusted income levels $18,000 and under. It should increase the loan limit to $2,500 per academic year and encourage the development of institutional and bank relationships that will provide incentives to promote the effective operation of the loan program, facilitate collections, and reduce unreasonable default rates. Work-study subsidies should be continued as a companion program to grants and loans.

Recognizing the great impact of the veterans' educational benefits on access and indirectly on the financing of postsecondary education, the federal government should plan increases in the Basic Educational Opportunity Grants Program to offset the losses in equality of student access that will result as veterans' benefits are phased out.

In addition to the access problem, the preservation of private institutions is another major issue in shaping financial policy. While private institutions have continued to grow in overall enrollment, their enrollments have declined steadily in proportion to all higher-education enrollments. Rising costs have forced private institutions to raise tuitions at a rate substantially faster than their public counterparts, creating what commonly has become known as the *tuition gap*. This phenomenon is believed to be a principal cause of the current decline in enrollments among private institutions, further reducing their share of total enrollments. There is considerable concern that this soon might result in closing a significant number of private institutions. The proponents of tuition increases for public schools indicate that such action would reduce the tuition gap and improve the competitive tuition position of private institutions. Studies do show that when tuition for public schools increases, more students tend to enroll in private institutions.

While I agree with the character of the problem and acknowledge the feasibility of the solution proposed, I disagree with the approach because of my strong feelings about the reasons for low tuition and because the tuition-gap problem can be solved by lowering private-institution tuitions through a variety of mechanisms. I believe that net tuition in private institutions should be reduced as rapidly as possible so that the range of private net tuition is lowered from the 1971–1972 level of 2.5 to 4.5 times to a level of 1.5 to 3.5 times that of net tuition in public four-year colleges and universities.

I believe this can be accomplished by a combination of several efforts:

(1) State assistance to private institutions. I believe as a matter of principle that private institutions not only should be recognized by each state as essential educational resources, but also that they should be considered in planning the basic institutional capability required in each state. In cases where enrollments still are expanding, assistance to private institutions may be in fact less expensive to the state than providing public institutional capacity.

(2) Modification of the Basic Educational Opportunity Grant Program, as indicated earlier, to remove the actual barriers to participation in this program by students attending private institutions.

(3) Modification of the guaranteed student loan program, as described earlier.

(4) Continued efforts to effect productivity gains in all institutions.

Reform and innovation are major items of concern in the development of financial policy. Every major report on postsecondary-education policy, and almost every conference, points to rising costs and the need for flexible and satisfying learning opportunities, curricular relevance, and productivity gains in the educational process. General opinion agrees that the process can be improved, the quality of educational output can be enhanced, educational substance can be more relevant to individual needs, and more students can be educated —if not for less money, at least not for more money. There is the feeling that if we just systematize and standardize, we can be more efficient and at the same time provide more flexible, creative, and imaginative arrangements for learning.

Our critics, very often our supportive critics, want increased credit-hour production, individualized instruction, higher student satisfaction, greater relevance, and competency-based learning—all for less money. Little evidence exists that all of these highly commendable desires are mutually supportive. For example, some of us have been studying the outputs of higher education very hard only to find that programs increasing productivity in the quantitative sense often decrease productivity in the qualitative sense. We must find an appropriate balance among conflicting, though commendable, objectives.

The methods of promoting reform and innovation are, of course, a matter of some debate. Promoters of higher public tuition also advocate increasing the flow of funds through the student, a plan designed to give students greater opportunity to "vote with their feet." This course would provide institutions with incentive for more response to student desires and theoretically would be an incentive to the desired reforms, assuming that students know what reforms they want and are good judges of what should be.

I concur that students may have a desirable impact on reform and innovation, but I do not concur that funds necessarily must flow through the students to achieve that end. It is possible to get the same effect by linking appropriations to enrollments. For example, by linking state funds for instructional services and programs to enrollments, the institutions and programs that most attract the students would get the support.

There are other ways to encourage and support reform, and they should not be overlooked in the debate about whether aid should be channeled through students. The federal government should provide grants to states and institutions that will make it possible for institutions to alter their instructional and managerial practices in response to major social and educational change. The government should review, update, and fund legislation to stimulate cooperative networks and centers. The federal government should act also to promote a stability of financing postsecondary education by adopting some general guidelines for shared financing responsibility and by appropriating federal funds sufficiently in advance of disbursement to allow students, institutions, and states to plan effectively.

For their part, institutions should improve productivity, both qualitative and quantitative, so that the rise in the cost of education does not exceed the general inflation rate. In addition, institutions and systems of postsecondary education, individually and collectively, should respond positively to the new public expectations for accountability. Postsecondary institutions should develop methods of communicating cost information to laymen in terms that they can understand. These institutions should determine and communicate the outputs or values of higher education and economize by sharing high-cost, underutilized resources. Postsecondary schools should modify allocation of resources to curricular and discipline areas in response to concerns for relevance. And, as an overriding concern, these schools should modify the educational process to enhance the ability of individuals to learn.

Research and graduate education are a major area of concern in the formation of financial policy. Among the factors influencing policy are the underemployment and unemployment of doctoral-degree holders, changing national priorities for research and manpower, declining enrollments, and the reduction of federal support for research and graduate education. The issue is not whether priorities should change or whether there should be a reasonable match between manpower needs and manpower training, but rather how to maintain, during a time of changing priorities and reduction of support, long-range research capacity and an adequate level of highly trained manpower. Research and graduate education capabilities are not built overnight. To let them lapse and then to restore them when we need them is likely to be costly and slow at a crucial time. Maintaining these capacities is a national interest.

Accordingly, the federal government should support selectively, through direct institutional grants and contracts and through aid to graduate students, high-quality research and graduate education in order to develop the nation's intellectual resources and to identify and resolve problems of national concern and priority. Federal support for institutional research and for graduate education, while adjusting to the priorities and levels of basic research support, should assure, in cooperation with the states and major research universities, a sustained capability to respond effectively to national research needs. In addition, the federal government should support, through institutional and student grants, a limited number of high-priority professional fields of study and training that are linked directly to national needs and concerns.

Another area that strongly affects financial policy is the emerging concept of postsecondary education as an interrelated enterprise. Congress has acted to include a host of noncollegiate institutions in federal financing arrangements and both the federal government and the National Commission on the Financing of Postsecondary Education are encouraging general recognition and acceptance of these institutions.

Many concerns still linger, however: With shortages of resources, will sharing them across more institutions and more students only compound financial problems and increase competition? Should institutions that offer such specialized job-oriented programs be considered for financial support on the same basis as traditionally accredited institutions? Are ethical problems involved because most of the noncollegiate institutions are profitmaking? Are students getting good instruction? How can the consumer be protected from abuses?

Partially allaying these concerns, the evidence shows that these institutions offer programs desired by students, though often at prices higher than those at public institutions offering the same programs. Noncollegiate institutions respond rapidly to demands of students for specialized job training, are improving accrediting and consumer-protection arrangements, and are willing to work with the collegiate institutions in making available to citizens a broader spectrum of educational programs and settings. While it is too early to evaluate the problems and promises of the concept of postsecondary education, it is clear that we must encourage the recognition of learning wherever it takes place—in public or private, profit or nonprofit settings. Furthermore, we should develop financing arrangements consistent with the profitmaking status of many of these institutions, permitting students who seek education in these settings to receive financial assistance if necessary.

A final area of concern—and one that should be included in any consideration of financial policy—is private giving. Philanthropic support of higher education historically has been strong and consistent. As we move toward a broader concept of postsecondary education, with an increasing portion of the enterprise turning public, there may be a tendency for private sources to assume that public funds will do the job. However, funds from private sources are especially important for they are often undedicated, providing programing flexibility that adds varying texture to the qualities of learning experiences available.

Private support—whether from alumni, foundations, organizations, or individuals—should not only be sustained but expanded. To encourage this, federal and state governments should maintain appropriate tax incentives. At the same time, contributors to postsecondary education should be encouraged to include unrestricted gifts in their donations, permitting maximum flexibility in the use of such income and preserving institutional integrity.

At this point, it is proper to ask whether the necessary resources will be forthcoming to carry out the policies outlined here. The current popular opinion and my own impressions of the reports of the Carnegie Commission and the views of the Committee for Economic Development are that we cannot expect significant increases in public support for postsecondary education. Indeed, the National Commission on the Financing of Postsecondary Education has acknowledged that the share of state revenues allocated to postsecondary education has declined recently. This trend is not likely to be reversed if basic attitudes and priorities continue. However, these predictions were made at a time when data were not yet available to show a general increase in state revenues and an increase in state appropriations for postsecondary education, even though the appropriations still were a declining portion of total state revenues. Further, the predictions were made at a time when the energy crisis was not widely anticipated, and even now we find it difficult to predict how that may affect financing.

While I cannot speculate on the vagaries of the economy, I am somewhat more optimistic than most experts about the ability of postsecondary education to obtain a reasonable share of the public resources available. I believe the American people and their elected representatives genuinely support postsecondary education. They see the need for higher education and want it adequately supported. However, they often are very vocal, and at odds with those of us intimately involved in the process, about what postsecondary education ought to be, whom it should serve, and how it should do so.

The public recognizes its own lack of expertise and does not feel it should bring about changes, but rather expects the experts to cause the changes. Since change has not occurred in accordance with the people's expectations, based on limited information available to them, people increasingly are asking for information that will explain to them why what we currently are doing is right and worthy of their support and what other things could be done that would be better. This situation provides me with some hope that public attitudes toward support of postsecondary education can be improved by bringing about changes in postsecondary education consistent with public expectations, providing information that demonstrates the value and efficiency of postsecondary education, or both.

All of us have reason to be challenged by the future, not by virtue of how great things are going to be, but rather by the opportunities we have to address some difficult but possible tasks. We all have talked about how we would like to become involved in meaningful reform and innovation. Well, our opportunity has come. The demand for reform is here.

25

What Is Left to Govern?

Harold L. Enarson

In some arcadia found only in treasured memory or in the poor remembrance of things past, there exists—like a flower frozen in amber—the autonomous, free-standing American state university. Perhaps in the McKinley or Coolidge era, the state university stood proud, free, independent. Presumably a statehouse clerk in green eyeshade delivered a sack of dollars once each biennium and then turned away shyly for the next two years while the university, in enjoyment of its autonomy, proceeded in its fashion.

Such caricature contains trace elements of truth. The typical state university of a generation ago did operate in a world relatively free of external constraints. The university president in the 1940s dealt

162

with few accrediting agencies; he was a stranger to federal guidelines and affirmative-action programs. The president had not been introduced to the many constraints imposed by state coordinating boards, nor did he even contemplate the special delights of bargaining collectively with several unions—including a union of the faculty itself. The university president was innocently unaware of the management help that would soon be contributed by state auditors, state architects, state civil-service boards, state coordinating and/or controlling boards, and well staffed standing committees of the state legislature.

It is tempting to envy the university administrators of a past now only dimly remembered: no computer printouts of student credit-hour costs, no thick reports on student station use, no cost centers in the medical college, no hopelessly technical calculations of indirect costs and research overhead, no abstruse arguments over the definitions of an F.T.E. faculty and F.T.E. students.

In those halcyon days of treasured independence, it is remembered that university presidents dealt frequently with faculty and occasionally with honest-to-God students. The student personnel movement had not developed; faculty and administrators naively believed that counseling students was largely the duty of faculty. For students in occasional trouble, we had a sex-oriented system—namely, a strong dean of men and an even stronger dean of women. It would be unfair to say that typically the dean of women and the dean of men were unlettered in matters of legal rights or untrained in psychology. To put it charitably, the deans operated much as Judge Roy Bean once operated on the banks of the Pecos River. Malefactors were dealt with summarily. Justice was swift and tempered occasionally with mercy. No appeals, thank you.

But enough of reminders of happier days—happier, that is, for those captains and sergeants of erudition who made up the administration. Today our publicly supported institutions of higher learning operate under a thick web of constraints and controls unknown in earlier times. Simply to list some of these newer constraints is to suggest the range and variety of unfamiliar intrusions into the internal life of the university:

(1) Our systems for record-keeping are increasingly dictated by various federal agencies, whether in personnel matters, the handling of radioactive waste, the policing of human subject research, or the accounting for faculty time on federal agency research projects.

(2) State civil-service laws and agencies create a special group, the civil service, with its own distinct salary, leave, and retirement subsystem.

(3) The architectural design, financing, and bidding of new buildings and the renovation of old buildings on campus is likely to be a bureaucratic obstacle course.

(4) Personnel controversies that were once resolved intramurally now move almost inexorably into a maze of commissions and courts, with the hapless institution sometimes caught in conflicting, even competing, jurisdictions.

(5) Entirely new legislation, such as the Occupational Safety and Health Act, imposes new restrictions with the burden of added costs.

(6) Specialized accrediting agencies nibble critically at the university and with the best of intentions "cannibalize" the university.

(7) Finally, as if to usher in 1984, universities and even groupings of universities are consolidated under a state superboard while state coordinating boards are transmuted into centralized control systems.

Thus have external controls and constraints, rules, regulations, and procedures descended upon the once autonomous university.

We in the university world have watched this accumulation of external authority over the life of the university in moods ranging from vague disquiet to near despair. Recently we have witnessed an acceleration in the imposition of external controls. All this has created a literature that is rich with the language of lamentation. We speak sadly of outside *intervention,* of *intrusions* into internal affairs, of the *erosion* of autonomy, of the *homogenization* of higher education, of the *excesses* of centralization. We lay full claim to the pejorative phrase and saturate our lamentations with emotion-riddled words such as *red tape, bureaucracy, politicization,* and the like.

In all this, clarity of thought would be served if we were to distinguish between the rhetoric of debate and political squabble on the one hand and the reality of substantive issues on the other hand. It may be good debating tactics for universities to talk of *state bureaucrats,* just as it is good tactics for state-system people to talk about institutional *insularity, narrow local perspectives,* and the like. But such rhetoric does not help us to grapple well with immensely difficult issues.

No state-supported institution exists apart from the state which created it and whose public interest the institution exists to serve. By the same token, no state coordinating agency or any other government agency serves the goals of efficiency, economy, and accountability unless it has a sophisticated and sensitive grasp of the transcendent importance of quality education in all its rich and varied meanings.

We should expect that the individual university would have legitimate concerns about the kinds of intervention it experiences at the hands of external authority. But the state agency overseeing higher education also has equally legitimate concerns. The public charge of the state system generally includes the wise use of resources, improved delivery of educational services to neglected constituencies and communities, the fair pricing of education, and the balanced development of all the constituent units that make up a state system. Both the university and the state-system agency are accountable to the public through their elected representatives. If the state agency intrudes in institutional affairs, as it frequently does, the university may intrude in the domain of the state agency by actions that conflict with public obligations imposed on the agency. Any unbridled provincialism on the part of the university is as threatening to the public interest as the desire of state agencies to police universities for the sake of control.

The task ahead is to develop consultative relationships that bring the legitimate concerns of the individual institutions and the legitimate concerns of state agencies into shared perspectives. Warfare is too costly. In most states, both the universities and the state higher-education agency share, at the deepest level of conviction, multiple goals of equity, efficiency, economy, excellence, pluralism, diversity, and the like. Our conflicts—intense and passionate as they seem—are hardly civil wars. Rather, they are lover's quarrels by persons who see many things differently but who unite in strong conviction that higher learning is our mutual concern and responsibility. Some state control of public higher education is inescapable, just as some substantial degree of institutional independence is indispensable. Our collective task is to mesh the various interests. Wars of maneuver are poor substitutes for responsible, creative statecraft.

Our would-be controllers should take to heart our lectures on the tyranny of excessive centralization and thoughtless intrusion. But those of us serving in the universities should take to heart the admonition that we cease our lamentations and take a firmer hand in attacking those matters that are unmistakably within our direct responsibility.

What is left on campus to govern? The question almost invites a cynical response. In moods of exhaustion, a president is tempted to say that he is left with all the distasteful tasks of governance: to divide a starvation budget equitably, to pacify a restless student body, to telephone the mayor or governor or National Guard to quell the streakers, to mediate intramural controversies, and to put a fair face on the disaster of a losing athletic team. However, as John Gardner has so often emphasized, these large systems within which we spend our working lives contain much more elbow room for personal initiative than we dare admit, especially to ourselves.

So what is left to govern? *Just about everything:* The lump sum appropriation is fairly common; we have the necessary legal freedom to alter priorities in the division of resources. Faculty and deans and vice presidents are not hired or fired by superboards; this is our sweet privilege. The humane and efficient management of our dormitory systems is our task alone; no superboard would have it otherwise. The initiative for seeking research grants, foundation largesse, and private fund raising is exclusively ours. The demotion of losing coaches is everyone's interest but the exclusive burden of the president and/or the trustees. The organization of curricula and courses of instruction is still our domain, as are methods of instruction and measures of student performance. We are free to reorganize our administrative structure, consolidate departments, create centers and institutes, pioneer in interdisciplinary ventures, and join in interinstitutional cooperative ventures. As for the tenure system, this briar patch is ours to enjoy or modify as we wish.

What else is in our domain? We are free to revitalize liberal education, shorten the curricula, revise subject matter requirements, and even to alter drastically the internal system of governance. We are free, thankfully, to choose the textbooks, the library materials, and the laboratory equipment we desire; free to alter the standard tests used for admission to professional schools; free to open classes in the evening; free to combat excesses of specialization; and free to run bars, restaurants, bookstores, art galleries, sports programs, alumni tours, overseas excursions, and all those other good things.

Perhaps we have more freedom, even with all the constraints, than we have the talent, courage, and imagination to exercise. We are free to enforce the no-smoking signs in the classroom, to require full work for full pay, to equalize teaching loads, to police the manifest abuses of our grading systems, to improve space utilization by using late afternoon hours for instruction, to recruit minorities (at least for the present) and even to expel star athletes who flunk Physical Education 101.

What else is left to govern? Only educational policy in virtually every aspect—that's all. We can despair in the face of the dreary statistics on the new depression in higher education, or we can change those educational policies and practices which deny working people of all ages equal access to educational opportunity and deny ourselves the market that we need to sustain enrollments.

We can deplore the current emphasis on career training as the triumph of mere vocationalism, or we can fashion much improved counseling services with planned work-study experiences. There is simply no good reason why the world of work and the world of formal classroom instruction cannot be melded in creative ways which permit the student to test job interests while experiencing the relevance, or lack of relevance, of formal classroom instruction.

We can limp along with the present system of requirements for a baccalaureate degree or we can critically examine our systems—more likely nonsystems—and find ways to save everyone's time. Something is terribly wrong when a typical student requires four and one-half years to complete a standard four-year program. Yet this waste of time is now generally the common experience.

We can cherish our few remaining overseas projects, lament the new isolationism of our nation, deplore the fading interest of the foundations and the federal government in promoting an international dimension—or we can redefine our academic requirements to include a far more vivid sense of the diversity of world cultures and our mutual dependence. The familiar incantations in defense of a foreign-language requirement intone the symbols rather than the substance of cross-cultural understanding.

We can be timorous in the face of collapsing standards and intellectual sloth, or we can insist that the fifty-minute classroom hour require intellectual rigor from teacher and student alike; that the grading system be fair and equitable; that the syllabus be coherent and relevant—and that it be honored; and that the teaching-learning enterprise be infused throughout with an insistence on high quality performance.

Let's face it—the agenda is crowded with tasks that are solely within the competence and concern of the individual college or university. In these great domains no state agencies constrain us, intrude upon us, or dictate to us.

Sartre insisted that free men are "condemned to freedom." So it is with our colleges and universities. We are condemned to much more choice than we are prepared to acknowledge, let alone to face. It is much easier to rail at the insensitivity of "that world out there"—the governors, legislators, state bureaucracies, and an indifferent public—than it is to face up to the burden of choice.

But, it may be asked, "whose choice?" And there is the rub! Is educational change the inescapable responsibility of the administration, with the faculty in an advise and consent and support role? Or is that collective entity, the faculty, finally responsible for educational policy, with the administration in a supporting role? As things now stand, one wonders who in the university is accountable for what.

As is well known, faculty and administration stereotype one another, each imputing to the other more authority and less wisdom than in truth exists. The result is that most changes are at the margins. Change does come, but it comes slowly, haltingly, clumsily. Much of the time our universities are in a state of *dynamic immobility* (a phrase borrowed from the rector of a Latin-American university). It is not that we are static—far from it. Powerful forces are at work, but these invite resistance from equally powerful counterforces: thus we are dynamic *and* immobile.

All this makes for easy evasion of responsibility. There is always a *they* standing between us and the changes we most want to make. There may be no ideal distribution of power and influence and responsibility within a university, but only makeshift accommodation in the context of interests forever in conflict.

And yet there are some old truths which deserve reaffirmation. The complications in governance that so frustrate the administrator and baffle the outside observer grow out of a very special, little understood aspect of teaching. Faculties are like policemen on the beat—admittedly an observation destined to antagonize both tribal groups. Both are "reverse discretion" hierarchies.[1] In the typical bureaucracy, organization is hierarchical; policy is developed at the top and refined at each level as it moves downward to the imposition of a control or the delivery of a service. But cops and professors enjoy an extraordinarily wide range of discretion precisely at the point of control or delivery.

---

[1] I am indebted to Dr. James (Dolph) Norton, chancellor of the Ohio Board of Regents, for the useful reminder of a key concept in organizational theory. This definition helps explain why chiefs of police and college presidents enjoy careers easily brought to abrupt endings.

Perhaps this is why both groups are skeptical, if not openly contemptuous, of supervision and control from headquarters. So too this is why in the special world of the university no basic reform or change is possible without faculty support and understanding.

I realize that exhortation went out of style with Teddy Roosevelt; if this is exhortation, make the most of it. The superboards won't destroy higher education; the Congress of the United States won't save it; and national blue-ribbon commissions won't chart our destinies. Change is now the most stable element of our times and alienation is its deadly companion. The machinery for participation—for governance, if you will—exists today on the North American campus. What does not exist is enough people who care and are willing to work for their convictions.

In cruel mimicry of contemporary American politics, the free citizens of academia know in their hearts that not much can be done about anything. And so believing, they make it come true. What is left to govern is ourselves.

Index